HEAVEN ON HORSEBACK

THE

WESTERN
EXPERIENCE

SERIES

☼

☼ ☼ ☼

☼ ☼ ☼ ☼ ☼

HEAVEN ON HORSEBACK

Revivalist Songs and Verse
in the Cowboy Idiom

☼ ☼ ☼ ☼ ☼

AUSTIN and ALTA FIFE

With a Preface by
William A. Wilson

Utah State University Press
Logan, Utah

Library of Congress Cataloging-in-Publication Data

Fife, Austin E.
  Heaven on horseback: revivalist songs and verse in the cowboy
idiom / Austin and Alta Fife; with an introduction by William A.
Wilson.
    p. cm. — (Western experience series)
  ISBN 0-87421-044-5 :
    1. Revivals—Hymns. 2. Cowboys—Songs and music—History and
criticism. 3. Cowboys—Poetry. 4. Hymns, English—West (U.S.)
I. Fife, Alta Stephens. II. Title. III. Series: Western
experience.
BV460.F5   1989
264'.2'088636—dc20   89-22750
                                                       CIP

Cover design by Richard Firmage

Preface

It was with great pleasure that I learned of Utah State University Press's decision to reprint Austin and Alta Fife's last major folksong publication, *Heaven on Horseback: Revivalist Songs and Verse in the Cowboy Idiom* (1970). One of the Fifes' most important yet least-known studies of cowboy songs and poetry, *Heaven on Horseback* deserves much broader circulation among students of the American West and of American folklore in general.

Though the Fifes conceived of themselves primarily as regionalists—as collectors, archivists, and interpreters of western American traditions—their studies of these traditions always carried broader, national implications. For example, their *Saints of Sage and Saddle: Folklore among the Mormons* (1956) did indeed enlarge our understanding of the Mormon West.[1] Perhaps more important, it helped demonstrate that a vigorous American folklore could develop not just from transplanted, old-world traditions but from historical dramas enacted on native American soil. Their *Forms upon the Frontier: Folklife and Folk Arts in the United States* (1969, with Henry Glassie)[2] did, to be sure, bring to light certain western folk genres, but it also inspired interest in American material culture that would soon spread across the land. And their publications of western verse and folksong helped delineate not just western American character but also a national identity shaped by life on America's ever-expanding frontier.

The Fifes began the work that would lead to these folksong publications in the late 1930s, when Austin was a graduate student at Stanford University serving as a research assistant to the distinguished scholar of Hispanic-American folklore, Aurelio Espinosa. During breaks and vacations from graduate study in an attempt to apply the methodology of folklore to their own Mormon and western cultural heritages, the Fifes began criss-crossing the West, gathering first the materials that would lead to the publication of *Saints of Sage and Saddle* and then expanding their collecting efforts to western folksongs. Two decades later, under a Guggenheim Fellowship, they visited libraries and archives across the entire country, assembling a manuscript collection to complement their abundant field recordings. In a 1972 interview, Austin described the nature of this collection, now housed in the Utah State University Folklore Archives, and its significance for research:

> We've talked to hundreds of people, and we've recorded this material, and the study comprises the archival form [of] those interviews and library research. . . . And it involves principally an index of western and cowboy song which comprises bound volumes of actual transcriptions, stenographic, or machine, or otherwise. It involves the tapes that we have actually made in the field. It involves the 4 x 6 comprehensive index [cards] bringing all those materials together and all of the books or other published encounters with those songs. So, for example, I could go to let's say "The Strawberry Roan" . . . and pull out one hundred 4 x 6 cards which will give me every manifestation of "Strawberry Roan" that I have . . . [encountered] in my life's career as a researcher—a singer in the field, a book, an LP recording, an old 78 r.p.m. recording, any of them at all. . . . I would have every manifestation that I have encountered, every article that's been written that's critical about it, every remark a politician has made about it, if it made print, and so on—it's there. And the back-up is there, either in our bound volumes from our field collecting . . . or in the tapes that we have made . . . [of] the actual singing. And by the way, all the tapes, nearly, have been transcribed into musical notation.[3]

From this assembled material the Fifes had hoped to create something of a cowboy epic. According to their friend, folklorist Wayland Hand, they believed

> that in its own beauty and grandeur, when all the cowboy materials are pieced together, you would have an equivalent of a grand epic of the American cowboy—attested to in thousands of verses, floating verses that if properly analyzed and brought together would constitute something that would be comparable to Homer's epic.[4]

When their hopes of completing this magnificent endeavor were cut short by Austin's failing health, the Fifes began to share their materials through a series of anthologies. First came a richly annotated republication in 1966 of N. Howard "Jack" Thorp's 1908 volume, *Songs of the Cowboy,* the first collection of cowboy songs published in the United States.[5] The comparative analyses, cultural/historical commentaries, notes, and lexicons provided by the Fifes for each of Thorp's twenty-three songs push the fifty pages of the original work to some 350 pages and give good insight into the Fifes' exacting scholarship.[6]

Next, in 1969, came the magnificent *Cowboy and Western Songs: A Comprehensive Anthology,*[7] which includes songs covering a full range of experiences from life in the West before the cowboy's arrival to the fading of the frontier and his disappearance from the scene, and which must remain a starting point for serious study of cowboy and western lore. The Fifes' comments on the sources for their work reveal once again their rich field and archival experience and a demanding methodology that did not allow the creating of composite texts or tampering with the actual creations of the singers, for whatever ends:

> The songs offered here have been selected from among several thousand possible choices: all the previously published collections, plus some forty volumes of notes and transcriptions of field recordings made by the authors and their colleagues in a dozen western states. For each song, we have chosen from among many variants one or more texts that ring truest to the cowboy mode. We have not made up "synthetic" texts by combining the "best" stanzas from sundry sources, although, in a few cases where the text selected is defective, we have offered stanzas from other sources with clear indication that the stanza (or stanzas) in question is not integral to the text it accompanies.[8]

The anthology was followed in 1970 by *Ballads of the Great West,*[9] a collection this time not of songs but of cowboy poetry, though many of the poems included had moved in and out of the sung tradition. The book is important not just because it further illuminates the circumstances of cowboy and western life but because it focuses on works intended for recitation and thus anticipates the development of the Cowboy Poetry Gathering, which each year draws thousands of working cowboys and cowboy buffs to Elko, Nevada, to regale each other with recitations of their poetry.

The year 1970 also marked the publication of the Fifes' final cowboy folksong and poetry collection—the little volume at hand, *Heaven on Horseback.* Some of its forty-nine songs and poems have been published in the earlier works, though well over half appear here for the first time. What is new, however, is not so much the material but the Fifes' approach to it.

Many scholars have been aware of the interplay, the borrowing back and forth, between cowboy verse and the fundamentalist and revivalist religious hymns the cowboys brought with them to the West, but few have written systematically on the subject, and no one has shown how cowboys have created in their poems and songs an idealized representation of the world they cherish here—heaven on horseback. That is the singular achievement of this volume. Cowboys have sung songs and recited poems on a spate of subjects, but by looking only at those that focus on life beyond "the last round-up," after a cowboy has saddled up his "faithful old pony" for the last time, has crossed the "big divide" and headed for the "home corral," the Fifes bring us closer to cowboy hearts and minds than we are likely to come through most other means—and closer also, perhaps, to the ideals and values that keep the cowboy in a central position in America's pantheon of heroes.

What we get from the songs and poems is a reflection not just of cowboy values but, as noted above, of those characteristics we have tended to call American. First of all, the cowboy is a typical American frontier hero: ruggedly independent and self-reliant, a lover of freedom, honest, courageous, rough and uncouth in manners and social graces, but always gentle to women (especially mothers), and a defender of religious values, though not of the institutionalized church. Like the logger, the railroader, and the oil driller, he is also a typical nineteenth-century American occupational hero, an exemplar of the Protestant Ethic: hard working, honest to the core, generous "to the man that's down," loyal to the outfit ("to the brand") and especially to boon companions, for whom he will sacrifice his own life at the drop of a hat.

The cowboy hero is the sum of all these parts, but he is also more than the sum. He is a quality, an essence; he is cowboy—his love of freedom totally unremitting, his closeness to nature and to God in nature profoundly moving, his isolation and loneliness both hurting and healing ("We want the night sound of cricket and owl,/ We want to get lonesome when coyotes howl"), his dry, self-deprecating sense of humor saving. Belonging to "a passel o' men what ain't no saints," he is finally too true to himself ("Brand me just what I am—an' I'm just what you see") ever to enter heaven on any but his own terms. Beyond that great divide, he must have his horse, his pals, his expansive western landscape, his cattle to herd, and, at last, his integrity ("Tell 'em I'll stay on th' range, but if I'm shut outside/ I'll abide it like a man because I ain't no quitter;/ I ain't going to change just when I cross th' Big Divide").

The Fifes speak frequently of "the myth of the cowboy." They are not speaking of something false but rather of something fundamentally true—a complex of images and symbols growing out of, reflecting, strengthening, and influencing the way both cowboys and others perceive and relate to this larger-than-life western hero. Whatever the actual reality of cowboys and the cowboy world, the enduring mythic cowboy remains a fundamental part of the American psyche—from the Marlboro Man to the Cowboy Poetry Gathering at Elko. And we all remain in Austin and Alta Fife's debt for helping us better understand not just the cowboy, but ourselves.

William A. Wilson
Brigham Young University
October, 1989

Notes to Preface

[1]Austin and Alta Fife, *Saints of Sage and Saddle: Folklore Among the Mormons* (Bloomington: Indiana University Press, 1956; Magnolia, MA: Peter Smith, 1966; Salt Lake City: University of Utah Press, 1980).

[2]Austin and Alta Fife and Henry H. Glassie, eds., *Forms Upon the Frontier: Folklife and Folk Arts in the United States,* Monograph Series Volume XVI, Number 2 (Logan: Utah State University Press, 1969).

[3]Personal interview with Austin Fife, conducted by William A. Wilson, 31 May 1972.

[4]Personal interview with Wayland D. Hand, conducted by David Stanley, 16 June 1986.

[5]N. Howard Thorp, *Songs of the Cowboys* (Estancia, New Mexico: News Print Shop, 1908).

[6]N. Howard Thorp, *Songs of the Cowboys,* commentary, notes, and lexicon by Austin and Alta Fife (New York: Clarkson N. Potter, 1966).

[7]Austin and Alta Fife, *Cowboy and Western Songs: A Comprehensive Anthology* (New York: Clarkson N. Potter, 1969; New York: Bramhall House, 1982).

[8]Fife and Fife, *Cowboy and Western Songs.*

[9]Austin and Alta Fife, eds., *Ballads of the Great West* (Palo Alto: American West, 1970).

Heaven on Horseback

THE

WESTERN
EXPERIENCE

SERIES

Table of Contents

Acknowledgments

We are grateful to colleagues, friends, and institutions who have contributed the resources that have made this study possible. Especially we wish to thank T. Y. Booth, Mary Washington, William H. Ramsey, and Millard Wilde at Utah State University; Mary Jo Schwab and Michael R. Packham; Wayland D. Hand, D. K. Wilgus, and the Center for the Study of Comparative Folklore and Mythology at the University of California at Los Angeles; the Archive of Folk Song at the Library of Congress; the John Edwards Memorial Foundation; and Vice President D. Wynne Thorne and the Division for Research at Utah State University.

Introduction

Interplay between sacred music and secular music has been inevitable since the foundations of society were laid. The same tunes served the diverse needs of worship, laughter, work, or tears, and migrated freely from chapel to street, market, tavern, festival, vaudeville, occupational group, prison, or any other milieu of the folk. Texts, rhythms, and musical styles that did not fit a given environment were spontaneously adapted or mindfully reworked to accomplish the task at hand.[1] Even today if we think of sacred music at its most popular levels — that of fundamentalist and revivalist sects rather than of the cathedrals and metropolitan parishes of the prestigious churches—then sacred and secular singing is of one piece.

Although many have commented on the interaction between sacred and popular secular music in the frontier environment, we are not aware that any systematic investigations have been undertaken in this area.[2] The influence of traditional hymns as inspiration for cowboy songs has been recognized but not documented.[3] The reverse of the process, the influence of the cowboy idiom on revivalist music, has received little attention, although John A. Lomax's papers contain one folder of revivalist parodies of cowboy songs, indicating his awareness of the genre.[4] In this particular study we shall treat all aspects of religious musical expression in the cowboy idiom, although a number of related areas must be explored before a comprehensive statement can be made concerning the relationships of sacred and other popular secular music in the American West.

Meanwhile certain aspects of frontier life need to be kept in mind if we are to understand the sacred aspects of cowboy songs and the textures rendered to revivalist music by the cowboy idiom. First let it be said that hymns and other revivalist music moved west with homesteaders and cattlemen, and played an important role in their lives.[5]

Hymns were sung in cow camps and on trail drives, along with traditional and popular songs, and old timers have claimed that they were sung or hummed effectively on night herd to prevent stampedes.[6]

Spell cites an amusing trail drivers' parody to a favorite pioneer hymn "At the Cross":

> At the bar, at the bar
> Where I smoked my first cigar
> And my nickels and my dimes rolled away,
> It was there by chance
> That I tore my Sunday pants
> And now I can wear them every day.[7]

In this study we propose to explore the ways in which Anglo-American revival songs reshaped the conventional images which Westerners had previously entertained about ultimate reality until a whole new idiom was created: the image of life-after-death conceived as an idealized extension of the Western experience itself. This is, of course, not the first time that man has re-landscaped and re-staged the setting of heaven and the plot for salvation in conformity with the locale and circumstances of his earthly being. For the Hebrew prophets the post-mortal state was patriarchal, polygamous, and pastoral. To the ancient Greeks it was occupied by anthropomorphic gods whose militancy, muscular exploits, virility, and passions were magnifications of those of Hellenic society in the millennium before Christ. The Neo-Platonists of the Renaissance gave heaven the pageantry and sensuality of carnival or of Rabelais' *Abbey of Thélème* where free-choice, sensual indulgence, learning, the arts, and elegance almost obliterated Gregorian images of a god of retribution and a life of self-denial. Right here in America while Anglo-Westerners were packing their heaven with prairies, cattle ranges, roundups, and men on horseback, the American Negro was projecting an idealized eternity which would rectify all of the blemishes wrought in his soul by the degradations of slavery and privation. This they expressed in their revival meetings and through their magnificient spirituals, or in the brothels and prison work gangs through their overpowering blues and work songs. It suggests the Voltarian dictum about God being created in the image of man, for here indeed do we see heaven and the hereafter remolded to conform with man's reaction to human experience. In the same period the idiom of the railroads also came to serve as a model for the after-life, but that must be the subject for another study.

— 2 —

INTRODUCTION

In the songs and poetry forming the basis for this study, the landscapes of heaven are but glorified plots of the western cattle country —a land of green pastures and rolling hills where cattle graze untouched by adversity. Western badlands are viewed as protected areas to remind man of the way the earth was as God made it: a place void of the wounds left thereon by the white man's intrusions, where he can get away from his peers and come near seeing God himself. A dying cowboy—like faithful Moslems in the cult for their holy city—requests burial in a grave shared with his horse, and facing the West. The Westerner's image of heaven also includes the presence of Indians, coyotes, wolves, owls, cacti, and other symbolic frontier fauna and flora. The setting for the after-life is the "home corral," the "big," "great," or "new" corral; the "home ranch" or "ranch house in the sky"—a place of rest, reassurance, warmth, companionship, love, and security: reward for loneliness and isolation felt by cowboys on roundup, trail drive, or night herd.

The routine or range life goes on in heaven as it does on earth: grazing, trail driving, roundup, cutting, roping and branding, night herding, sleeping beneath the open sky, mad rides to head off a stampede of stars, and meals eaten at the celestial chuckwagon. The heavenly ranges are, of course, inhabited by the cowpoke's favorite horse: otherwise no self-respecting cowboy would care to go there. Celestialized cowboys ride over the heavenly ranges, tall in their golden saddles and throwing their golden-fibered lassoes on cloud-range cattle or the dogies of the Milky Way. These ranges of the hereafter are ridden by more ominous cowboys too: Riders of Judgment and wranglers in the employ of Old Nick himself.

Heaven is situated in the sky and west of the West: the passage from life to death is for ranch folk a ride over and beyond the Great Divide. Images for death emerge which are compatible with the new terrain and new modes of being in the West. Canyons and gorges loom as danger points which might cause a cowpoke to take the wrong trail, ending up in hell. The passage of men over this "glory trail" is analogous to the drives which took western dogies east to the railroads. The throes of death are likened to the milling of nervous cattle prior to stampede, and the human body divested of the soul is a shriveled thing —like the camp cook's curled bacon.

Mortals are wrangled along the trails of salvation by "Riders of Judgment" or by "Trail Riders" who once were cowboys, Saint Peter acting as the Final Owner's brand inspector. God himself, once a cowboy, is known variously as the "Big Boss," "Head Boss," "Sky Boss," "Ranch Boss," "Range Boss," "Trail Boss," "Trail Rider," the "Boss of the Riders," the "Foreman," or the "Great Owner." Satan, the anti-creator, is of cowboy breed too and is known variously as the "boss of the rustlers," the "other great owner." His "riders," "rangers," "rustlers" share tasks with God's riders at the last great roundup, receive the "cuts" or "tailings," and wrangle them away to their own ranges.

All of the cowboy's operations with respect to the handling of cattle are used metaphorically to designate God's or the devil's manipulations of the human herd: rounding up, trail driving, cutting, roping, branding, ear-marking, recording in the Tally Book. Mankind is to God as the cattle herd is to the ranch owner. The biblical metaphor where sheep symbolize men and the Savior is a shepherd is replaced by the image of God as owner, range boss, etc., and mankind as cattle, dogies, or—if sinful—strays, mavericks, "longhorn coasters" who suffer from "the mange of sin," or men gone astray under the spell of "locoed" doctrines. Life is a mad stampede followed by the big drive across the Great Divide where, at a "cutting and branding" administered jointly by the riders of the Big Boss and the "other great owner," the dogies will be cut and branded, their names recorded in the great Tally Book, and then driven on, some to the green pastures of the Big Owner's corral, and the others wrangled away to hell.

Biblical precedence is cited, moreover, for the whole cowboy ethic. Cowboys who have earned salvation through good deeds are rewarded in heaven with golden or silver replicas of their earthly accoutrements: saddles, spurs, lariats. In contrast, an empty saddle is a grim memento of a cowboy called prematurely to the Last Roundup. The frontier saloon is an earthly symbol of the devil's domain. Cards and poker chips, though typically symbols of evil, may also be used for good, and a cowman's check-book, like the Tally Book encountered earlier, may record his good deeds or his bad ones.

Death, the after-life, and salvation are omnipresent themes in this literature. The journey into eternity is but a final ride on a cattle trail leading over the Great Divide and on to the "ranges of heaven," the "home ranch," the "home corral" of the Sky Boss. This trail is narrow, precipitous, fraught with danger points where one can easily get lost or take the wrong turn. In an ill-defined neutral region there is a grand roundup or a cattle sale where the riders of judgment, acting both for God and the "other great owner," "cut," "rope," "brand," or "maverick" the human critters, hazing them away to their eternal abode, be it the ranges of heaven or of hell. One is wise to mount his sure-footed night horse for this final journey lest he end up with the "cuts," the "tailings," who will go to the "other big owner's" corrals.

For the purposes of this study we have utilized texts which have circulated in oral tradition or in the columns of western newspapers and other popular imprints: camp and gospel singing, 78 rpm records, radio emissions, collections of verse by "western" poets who have sung the "myth" of the West rather than their own foibles. Westerners have been literate from the beginning and their myths have been propagated in print as often as by word of mouth.

Forty-nine songs, together with meaningful variants, have been selected to illustrate the juncture of the cowboy and western metaphor with the revivalist idiom: enough, we think, to illustrate the phenomenon, although many more could be added. They are grouped under seven headings: groups I, II, and III (text 1 to 22) illustrate the ways in which revivalist concepts intrude in cowboy and western songs without their being converted thereby into bona fide hymns. In the songs of groups IV and V (texts 23 to 32) the increment of revivalism is so great that these songs might truly be considered as hymns. The texts of group VI illustrate the intrusion of cowboy and western metaphor into prayers or homiletic verse, most of which have poetic forms not far removed from song.

The cowboy idiom lost its *raison d'être* by the 1930's, and degenerated thereafter as a dominant mass media motif: it went "Hollywood." This is true for cowboy and western revivalist songs, witness the nine "decadent" texts of group VII, most of which date from the years immediately preceding World War II.

The focus of this study is upon the use of the cowboy idiom as an expression of religious and transcendental ideas rather than upon the music. Where melodies are available we have, of course, given them, and when striking metrical similarity to hymns has been noted, and in the absence of tunes for the cowboy songs themselves, we have given music for the hymns. Frequently the most desirable texts and the melodies available do not come from the same source. In such cases the reader cannot expect text and tune to synchronize wholly. He must make obvious accommodations, especially with regard to rhythmical elements, just as any folk singer spontaneously does in order to express the ideas with the "swing" he wants to give them. Such accommodations may involve either words or music. Though stressed words, stressed notes, and the melodic line are fairly stable, all else is like plastic to hold the aggregate together.

We also feel constrained to avoid a detailed analysis of prosody, style, and form. At the "grass"—or shall we say "folk"—roots of most of this material is the venerable ballad meter consisting of stanzas of four lines, *a* and *c* having four and *b* and *d* three metric feet. Lines *b* and *d* are usually rhymed. A simple linear melody would accommodate it. Frequently a double stanza, the above repeated, occurs accommodating a melodic line of twice the length. Songs and hymns of the folk already offer a few variations of this basic form: stanzas having four lines each with four metric feet often rhymed *aa/bb;* rhymed couplets with six metric feet. In sophisticated sacred music and in the poetry of professionals many innovations are wrought.

We wish to conclude this introductory statement with some reflections about folk song transmission and folk song transformation based on the implications of the study. It is important to keep in mind that the Anglo-American culture has always been complex and its evolution rapid. This is manifest in the marvelous variety of its popular lyrical expressions: themes of migration and colonization; lumberjacks, sodbusters, cowboys and Westerners, hillbillies; blues and work songs; railroading; spirituals and cowboy songs were propagated in the culture almost simultaneously, and the spill-over from one category to another has been recurrent, persistent, and extensive. Almost any individual in the culture will have had experience with more than one, if not several, of these themes. This is especially so of name singers of the era of 78 rpm recordings (1910 to World War II). They performed at revival meetings; they recorded and broadcast folk, revival, and popular songs of whatever provenience, reshaping them to fit the needs of every audience. It is hence more meaningful to study the emergence of a given song or "song cluster" in the totality of its complex environment than to define each mythic theme (cowboy, lumberjack, etc.) too narrowly, and then to study influences of one upon the other. To be more specific and to apply this generalization in this particular study, the content of cowboy songs and revival songs is to be viewed not as interplay between themes of two distinct cultures, but rather as interplay between two mythic motifs within a single frontier culture.

Notes to Introduction

[1] Sometimes the secular manifestations of sacred music had a satirical or malicious intent: more often such borrowings occurred simply because worship, sentimentality, work, and laughter are integral aspects of the behaviour of the folk. Bakhtin notes, for example, that the *Magnificat* was sung "to the tune of clownish street rigmaroles" (Mikhail Bakhtin, *Rabelais and His World.* Cambridge, Mass., The M.I.T. Press, 1968, p. 79.)

[2] Clifford J. Westermeier ("The Cowboy and Religion," in *The Historical Bulletin,* XXVIII [Jan. 1950], pp. 31-37) has written on the cowboy's religious attitudes generally and cites "The Cattleman's Prayer" and "Grand Roundup" [numbers 35 and 9 of this study] to make his points, but he does not otherwise speak of the relationships between cowboy songs and sacred music.

[3] Myra Hull, "Cowboy Ballads," *Kansas State Historical Quarterly* VIII (Feb. 1939), pp. 35-37. Margaret Larkin and Helen Black. *Singing Cowboy,* New York: Alfred A. Knopf. 1931, p. vii. Wayne Gard. *The Chisholm Trail,* Norman: University of Oklahoma Press, 1954, pp. 115-116.

[4] Archives of the Texas Historical Society: John A. Lomax papers, dossier #5671 (JL 430 in Fife American Collection).

[5] Edward E. Dale, *Frontier Ways,* Austin: University of Texas Press, 1959, pp. 211-231. J. Frank Dobie in interview with Fifes (FAC I 549, p. 6). N. Howard Thorp, "Banjo in the Cow Camps" (in N. Howard Thorp and Austin and Alta Fife, *Songs of the Cowboys,* New York: Clarkson N. Potter, 1966, p. 16). N. M. Clark, "God's Roundup: Texas Cowboys' Meeting 53 Years Old," *Saturday Evening Post,* March 1943.

[6] J. Frank Dobie, "Ballads and Songs of the Frontier Folk," *Publications of the Texas Folklore Society,* VI (1927), pp. 168-169. N. Howard Thorp, *op. cit.,* pp. 18-19. J. Frank Dobie in interview with Fifes (FAC I 549, pp. 2 ff). John A. Lomax, *Cowboy Songs and Other Frontier Ballads,* New York: Macmillan, 1938, xvi-xvii. Wayne Gard, *op. cit.,* ch. XV, pp. 242-250. Ramon F. Adams, *Best of the American Cowboy,* Norman: University of Oklahoma Press, 1957, p. 24.

[7] Lota May Spell, *Music in Texas,* Austin, 1936, pp. 65-68.

Sources and Abbreviations

Complete references accompany all texts and melodies from published sources used in this study. However, some materials are from esoteric local publications, newspapers and other periodical literature of the American West, sheet music and popular song folios, popular recorded music of the 78-rpm era, our own field recordings and those of fellow researchers who have contributed significant cowboy and western items, and sundry manuscript resources. These resources which are not accessible in good research libraries have been assembled and entered in the ten volumes of the Fife Mormon Collection (FMC) and the forty-two volumes of the Fife American Collection (FAC). Tapes (or acetate recordings of the earlier items) are preserved of all songs gathered from oral sources.

Large private collections, entered into the Fife Collection as integral volumes, are identified by appropriate independent abbreviations. The ones referred to in this volume are as follows:

Gordon-Oregon: one volume extracted from the papers of Robert W. Gordon at the library of the University of Oregon.

Hendren: seven volumes from the private collection of Stella M. Hendren of Kooskia, Idaho.

JL: three volumes extracted from the manuscript collections of John A. Lomax in the archives of the Texas Historical Society, Austin.

PC-F: one volume from the private collection of Edwin Ford Piper at the State University of Iowa.

PNFQ: three volumes from the manuscript collection of the Pacific Northwest Farm Quad, Spokane, Washington.

Songs

Part I

The Coexistence of Ruggedness and The Christian Ethic

Men on the western fringes of the country enjoyed a reputation for rowdiness, rough speech and manners, and a readiness for violence which seemed in direct conflict with gentler and more civilizing ethics of Western European Christian tradition. Defenders of the Western image did not deny this elemental primitiveness of their kind; on the contrary, they magnified the image, and then sought biblical and other arguments to support their claim. The hypocritical, effeminate, conscience-striken behavior of the Sunday-go-to-meeting citified male is neither virile nor godly. Men were meant to flex their muscles, to affront the elements, to discern right and wrong on sight, defending the one and avenging the other by spontaneous, immediate, and violent action.

The seven texts of Part I are all written by poets of no uncertain artistry. Their arguments are sharply drawn and defended with consummate skill. Imagery and metaphor are rallied effectively, and (No. 2 excepted) metric and stanzaic forms have a baroque kind of richness and ostentation well suited to the content of the poems.

This is certainly not folk poetry, but poetry written for the folk by poets of skill and by poets striving successfully to quarry the gems of the Western myth and offer them to the folk for their acceptance and use. Song No. 2, "The Cowboy's Soliloquy," has passed into oral tradition as one of the greatest songs in the cowboy and Western idiom.

No. 1. *The Bar-Z of a Sunday Night*

An outward stance of toughness pervades literature of the American West, both in its oral and published forms. But this did not come into conflict with frequent surges of spirituality: witness the mood of the Bar-Z punchers on a Sunday night. The three lines quoted in stanzas 5 and 6 are from a widely known hymn, "Yield Not to Temptation," written in 1868 by Dr. H. R. Palmer and first published in the *National Sunday School Teachers Magazine*. Music to the hymn is given here, though we have not found music for "The Bar-Z of a Sunday Night."

(Text: JL 290. John A. Lomax [*Songs of the Cattle Trail and Cow Camp,* New York: Macmillan, 1928, pp. 129-130] ascribes it to Percival Combes. Melody: *"Yield Not to Temptation," The Broadman Hymnal,* B. B. McKinney, ed., Nashville, Tennessee: Broadman Press, 1940, p. 338.)

"Yield Not to Temptation"

Yield not to temp-ta-tion for yield-ing is
sin, fight man-ful-ly on-ward, dark pas-sions subdue, look ev-er to Jes-us He'll car-ry you
through.

We ain't no saints on the Bar Z ranch
    It's said, and we know who 'tis —
The devil has hold of us, root and branch
    And uses us in his biz.

Still we ain't so bad, but we might be worse
    And you'd sure admit that's right

If you happened all unbeknown to us
 Come of a Sunday night.

The week day manners is stowed away
 The jokes and the card games halts
When Dick's old fiddle begins to play
 A-tunin' it ain't no waltz.

It digs for the things that is out of sight
 It delves through the toughest crust
It grips the heart strings and holds 'em tight
 Till we've got to sing or bust.

With a pipin' treble the kid starts in
 And, hell, how that kid can sing!
"Yield not to temptation, for yieldin' is sin,"
 He leads and the rafters ring.

"Fight manfully onward, dark passions subdue,"
 We shouts it with force and vim,
"Look ever to Jesus, He'll carry you through,"
 That's puttin' it up to Him.

We ain't no saints on the old Bar Z
 But many a time and oft
When the old fiddle's a-pleadin' "Abide with me"
 Our hearts get kinda soft.

And we make some promises there and then
 Which we keeps till we goes to bed
Which is the most could be asked of a passel o' men
 What ain't no saints, as I said.

No. 2. *Cowboy's Soliloquy*

  This is a remarkable example of cowboy realism where the frontier ethic of rugged individualism is defended on biblical precedent. Still, the brash assertion of self is bracketed with lyrical and spiritual images bespeaking dependency of the individual on mankind and on God. (Text: *Kansas Cowboy,* Dodge City, April 25, 1885, by Allen McCanless. Clifford P. Westermeier [*Trailing the Cowboy,* Caldwell, Idaho: Caxton Printers, 1955, pp. 263-264] cites it from the *Trinidad* [Colorado] *Daily Adventurer,* April 9, 1885. Melody A: Victor 21402, Carl T. Sprague. Melodies B and C: John A. Lomax, *Cowboy Songs and Other Frontier Ballads,* New York: Macmillan, 1938, pp. 67-70. Recovered many times from oral sources, from newspapers, on 78 rpm records, and in most printed collections of cowboy and western songs.)

Melody A. *The Cowboy*

All day o'er the prai-ries a - lone I ride, —— Not e - ven a dog to run by my side; My —— fire I kin - dle with chips gath - ered round, —— And boil my cof - fee with - out be - ing ground. Bread lack - ing leav - en I bake in a pot, And sleep on the ground for want of a cot; I wash in a pud - dle and wipe on a sack And car - ry my ward - robe all on my back.

Melody B. *The Cowboy*

All day long on the prai - rie I ride, Not
e - ven a hound dog to trot by my side; My
fire it is kin - dled with chips gath - ered round; I
boil my own cof - fee with - out be - ing ground, I
wash in a pool and I wipe on a sack, I
car - ry my ward - robe all on my back, For
want of an ov - en I cook in a pot, For
want of a bed I sleep on a cot.

All day o'er the prairies alone I ride,
Not even a dog to run by my side,
My fire I kindle with chips gathered round
And boil my coffee without being ground.

Bread lacking leaven I bake in a pot
And sleep on the ground for want of a cot,

— 13 —

I wash in a puddle and wipe on a sack
And carry my wardrobe all on my back.

My ceiling the sky, my carpet the grass,
My music the lowing of herds as they pass.
My books are the brooks, my sermons the stones,
My parson's a wolf on a pulpit of bones.

But then if my cooking ain't very complete,
Hygenists can't blame me for living to eat.
And where is the man who sleeps more profound
Than the cowboy who stretches himself on the ground.

My books teach me constancy ever to prize,
My sermons that small things I should not despise,
And my parson remarks from his pulpit of bone
That the Lord favors those who look out for their own.

Between love and me lies a gulf very wide,
And a luckier fellow may call her his bride,
But Cupid is always a friend to the bold
And the best of his arrows are pointed with gold.

Friends gently hint I am going to grief,
But men must make money and women have beef,
Society bans me a savage and dodge,
And Masons would ball me out of their lodge.

If I'd hair on my chin I might pass for the goat
That bore all sin in ages remote
But why this is thusly I don't understand
For each of the patriarchs owned a big brand.

Abraham emigrated in search of a range
When water got scarce and he wanted a change.
Isaac had cattle in charge of Esau
And Jacob "ran cows" for his father-in-law.

He started in business clear down at bedrock
And made quite a fortune by watering stock.
David went from night-herding and using a sling
To winning a battle and being a king.
And the shepherds when watching their flocks on the hill
Heard the message from heaven of "Peace and Good Will."

Melody C. *The Cowboy*

All day on the prai - rie in the sad - dle I ride, Not

e - ven a dog, boys, to trot by my side; My

fire I must kin - dle with chips gath - ered round, And

boil my own cof - fee with out be - ing ground. My

fire I must kin - dle with chips gath - ered round, And

boil my own cof - fee with - out be - ing ground.

No. 3. *A Christian Cowboy's Creed*

The studied primitivism of this text by James Barton Adams is but a thin veneer covering a lyrical outpouring of sensitivity to raw nature and communion with the cosmos. (John Bratt, *Trails of Yesterday.* Chicago: University Publishing Co., 1921, pp. 207-208.)

I am no profess'n' Christian of the sort the cities hold.
Haint been gathered with the chosen in the chosen's sacred fold.
An' I've never grown in spirit while a-thinkin' o' the way,
That the reckless unbelievers sin around me every day.
All the creed I try to practice is the ol' time Golden Rule.

Never hear no sacred music but the breezes fresh and cool;
An' the only church o' worship onto which my fancy clings
Is the outdoor church o' nature whar the Lord's a-runnin' things.

I can get more soothing comfort from the music o' the brooks
Than the preachers o' creation ever rassled out o' books;
An' the sighin' o' the breezes an' the singin' o' the birds
Brings a sort o' Christian feelin' you can never get from words.
There is sermons in the sunshine, there's a discourse in the flowers.
There is heavenly baptism in the gentle springtime showers.
There is life an' inspiration in the brooks an' in the springs,
Out in nature's sanctuary whar the Lord's a-runnin' things.

While I'm ridin' on the night herd, every star that gleams above
Seems a sparkling gem that's speaking o' the Master's kindly love.
An' the flashin' o' the lightnin' an' thunder's angry roar
Tells me o' the power majestic, o' the Being I adore.
When the storm in awful fury is a-bawlin' in its wrath,
Like as if it'd sweep the cattle jes' like feathers from its path,
I'm contented as the sage chicks underneath their mother's wings;
Out in nature's big cathedral whar the Lord's a-runnin' things.

When I hear the final summons, sent to tell me I mus' go
To the Round-up in the Heavens from the ranges here below
Not a song nor not a sermon nor a ceremonious play
Do I want in the perceedin's, when my body's laid away.
I would rather far be buried on the ranges all alone,
With the spot whar I'm sleepin' never marked by board or stone;
So's when Gabriel sounds his trumpet I kin rise and spread my wings
From the grassy slopes of nature, whar the Lord's a-runnin' things.

No. 4.   *From Town*

It will require a doctoral dissertation or two to unravel the maze
of cowboy boasting songs. In stanza three of this highly artistic text
precedent for the deviant ways of cowboys—even cattle rustling—is
cited in the lives of the Hebrew patriarchs and their kin. (Charles
Badger Clark, *Sun and Saddle Leather*. Boston: Richard G. Badger,
1922, pp. 47-49.)

> We're the children of the open and we hate the haunts o' men,
> But we had to come to town to get the mail.

And we're ridin' home at daybreak—'cause the air is cooler then—
    All 'cept one of us that stopped behind in jail.
Shorty's nose won't bear paradin', Bill's off eye is darkly fadin',
    All our toilets show a touch of disarray,
For we found that city life is a constant round of strife
    And we ain't the breed for shyin' from a fray.

      Chant your warwhoop, pardners dear, while the east turns
          pale with fear
      And the chaparral is tremblin' all aroun'
      For we're wicked to the marrer; we're a midnight dream
          of terror
      When we're ridin' up the rocky trail from town!

We acquired our hasty temper from our friend, the centipede,
    From the rattlesnake we learnt to guard our rights.
We have gathered fightin' pointers from the famous bronco steed
    And the bobcat teaching us reppertee that bites.
So when some high-collared herrin' jeered the garb that I was wearin'
    'Twasn't long till we had got where talkin' ends,
And he et his illbred chat, with a sauce of derby hat,
    While my merry pardners entertained his friends.

      Sing 'er out, my buckeroos! Let the desert hear the news.
        Tell the stars the way we rubbed the haughty down.
      We're the fiercest wolves a-prowlin' and it's just our
          night for howlin'
      When we're ridin' up the rocky trail from town.

Since the days that Lot and Abram split the Jordon range in halves,
    Just to fix it so their punchers wouldn't fight,
Since old Jacob skinned his dad-in-law for six years' crop of calves
    And then hit the trail for Canaan in the night,
There has been a taste for battle 'mong the men that follow cattle
    And a love of doin' things that's wild and strange,
And the warmth of Laban's words when he missed his speckled herds
    Still is useful in the language of the range.

      Sing 'er out, my bold coyotes! leather fists and leather throats,
        For we wear the brand of Ishm'al like a crown.
      We're the sons o' desolation, we're the outlaws of creation—
        Ee-yow! a-ridin' up the rocky trail from town!

No. 5. *The Raven Visits Rawhide*

Confrontations between God and Satan, or between saint and sinner, have been with us from the beginning. Here this dramatic episode is staged in a saloon, the parson and his flock coming in from the revival hall next door. The saloon keeper's blasphemous toast is countermanded when the self-styled "Raven," persuader in hand, steps out on the floor and forces the rowdy set to get down on their knees and pray. Still, the battle ends in ambivalence, the Raven riding off on the parson's horse with the money from the saloon keeper's till. (Hendren 446.)

It was meetin' night in Rawhide Town,
And the congregation was settlin' down
To hear the sermon of Parson Brown,
    When hell broke loose again.
Next door in Hank's Cafe Paree
The boss was off on his weekly spree,
And settin' 'em up to the cowmen free
    From a barrel of nigger gin.

The parson strained his lungs to shout,
But Hank's rejoicin' drowned him out,
The devil was winnin' without a doubt
    And heaven's hopes looked slim.
The parson paused, then shouted, "Men,
The time's at last appointed when
We'll beard the devil in his den,
    And have it out with him."

Out of the church with his little flock,
The parson p'raded down the block,
Lifted the latch without a knock,
    And entered the hall of sin.
The music ended, the laughter died,
Tongues went speechless and eyes grew wide,
As the parson calmly stepped inside,
    And the others followed in.

For an instant no one dared to speak,
Even the parson's knees were weak.
He'd forgot the vengeance he'd planned to wreak,
    And Hank looked on with a frown.

But Hank was not so easily downed,
He grabbed a glass and held his ground
And ordered the boys to drink a round
    To the parson of Rawhide Town.

"It's the bottoms up!" the barkeeper cried,
"We'll drink to hell where we'll all be fried,
Where we'll cast our souls that are crimson-dyed,
    In the tears our women shed."
The toast was drunk, then Hank stepped up,
Offered the parson a brimmin' cup,
And said, "Drink up, you prayin' pup,
    And trot on home to bed."

Hank laughed when suddenly out on the floor,
A stranger stepped with a '44—
And Hank was looking into the bore,
    And wond'ring what to do.
The stranger was lean and hard and small,
And he spoke words with a lazy drawl,
He said, "Now, boys, now listen all,
    And I'll have a word with you.

"I ain't the kind to be buttin' in,
And I'll prob'ly never be here again,
But, boys, I'm mad—I'm mad as sin,
    And I'm going to have my say.
Take my advice and don't get rough,
I'm called the Raven, and, boys, I'm tough,
If you think I ain't, jes' call my bluff,
    Now, pray, you buzzards, pray."

Down in the dirt on the rum-soaked floor,
The cowmen knelt till their knees were sore.
And they prayed as they'd never prayed before,
    To save their souls from hell.
And when the parson said amen,
They followed him out of the devil's den,
And they swore they'd be different men,
    But they crossed their fingers well.

The Raven and Hank were left alone,
And the Raven spoke in a gentle tone.

He said, "I'm sorry you pulled that bone,
    For your technique sure is bad!
My sole intentions in comin' here
Was merely to buy a round of beer,
And lift your roll, but now I fear
    I've run things in a ditch.

"So open your poke and spill the dough,
And I'm beggin' your pardon as I go
That I had to spoil your little show,
    'Cause our ideas didn't hitch."
Hank looked twice at the '44,
And decided he'd better act before
His guest became a trifle sore,
    So he shoved the roll across the floor.

The Raven bid him a soft good night,
Lifted his gun and blinked the light,
Slammed the door and was off in flight,
    Ridin' the parson's horse.

No. 6.   *Riders of the Stars*

There is epic grandeur, or else pure corn, in the image of ten thousand bow-legged cowboys in a protest march against God's own cherubim, demanding mounts and nightly exit from the confines of heaven to ride herd on the Milky Way, to rope maverick comets, and to roundup their herd in the corral of Saturn's rings. This range poet may have begun tongue-in-cheek, but the topic forthwith stampeded giving him a good run on a cosmic trail. The similarities between this poem and Rudyard Kipling's "Tomlinson" suggest that Mr. Knibbs was familiar with it when he wrote "Riders of the Stars." (Henry Herbert Knibbs, *Riders of the Stars,* Boston and New York: Houghton Mifflin Co., 1916, pp. 6-9.)

Twenty abreast down the Golden Street ten thousand riders marched;
    Bow-legged boys in their swinging chaps, all clumsily keeping time;
And the Angel Host to the lone, last ghost their delicate eyebrows
        arched
    As the swaggering sons of the open range drew up to the Throne
        Sublime.

— 20 —

Gaunt and grizzled, a Texas man from out of the concourse strode,
 And doffed his hat with a rude, rough grace, then lifted his eagle
  head;
The sunlit air on his silvered hair and the bronze of his visage glowed;
 "Marster, the boys have a talk to make on the things up here," he
  said.

A hush ran over the waiting throng as the Cherubim replied:
 "He that readeth the hearts of men He deemeth your challenge
  strange,
Though He long hath known that ye crave your own, that ye would not
  walk but ride,
 Oh, restless sons of the ancient earth, ye men of the open range!"

Then warily spake the Texas man: "A petition and no complaint
 We here present, if the Law allows and the Marster He thinks it fit;
We-all agree to the things that be, but we're longing for things that ain't,
 So we took a vote and we made a plan and here is the plan we
  writ:—

" *'Give us a range and our horses and ropes, open the Pearly Gate,*
 And turn us loose in the unfenced blue riding the sunset rounds,
Hunting each stray in the Milky Way and running the Rancho straight;
 Not crowding the dogie stars too much on their way to the bedding-
  grounds.

" *'Maverick comets that's running wild, we'll rope 'em and brand 'em*
  fair,
 So they'll quit stampeding the starry herd and scaring the folks
  below,
And we'll save 'em prime for the round-up time, and we riders'll all be
  there,
 Ready and willing to do our work as we did in the long ago.
                                                        ●

" *'We've studied the Ancient Landmarks, Sir; Taurus, the Bear, and*
  Mars,
 And Venus a-smiling across the west as bright as a burning coal,
Plain to guide as we punchers ride night-herding the little stars,
 With Saturn's rings for our home corral and the Dipper our water-
  hole.

" 'Here, we have nothing to do but yarn of the days that have long gone by,
And our singing it doesn't fit in up here, though we tried it for old-time's sake;
Our hands are itching to swing a rope and our legs are stiff; that's why,
We ask you, Marster, to turn us loose—just give us an even break!' "

Then the Lord He spake to the Cherubim, and this was His kindly word:
"He that keepeth the threefold keys shall open and let them go;
Turn these men to their work again to ride wih the starry herd;
My glory sings in the toil they crave; 'tis their right. I would have it so."

Have you heard in the starlit dusk of eve when the lone coyotes roam,
The *Yip! Yip! Yip!* of a hunting cry, and the echo that shrilled afar,
As you listened still on a desert hill and gazed at the twinkling dome,
And a viewless rider swept the sky on the trail of a shooting star?

No. 7.   *Theology in Camp*

That Silver Jack, who had not always "used the lord exactly right," should come to His defense in the face of an undisguised act of blasphemy is not inconsistent with frontier mentality. By its style and subject matter the poem evokes the bloody acts of carnage wrought against infidel Saracens by Bishop Turpin and the knights of Charlemagne on the marches of Spain (*Song of Roland*). There are conflicting claims to authorship and about the real-life circumstances which provoked its composition. (Quoted from Gordon-Oregon 77. His source, "Whitewater Bart," ascribes its composition to an incident in the spring of 1880.)

I was on the drive in eighty
Working under Silver Jack,
Which the same is now in Jackson
And ain't soon expected back.

And there was a chap among us
By the name of Robert Waite
Kind o' cute, and smart, and tonguey,
Guess he was a graduate.

He could talk on any subject
    From the Bible down to Hoyle,
And his words flowed out so easy,
    Just as smooth and slick as oil.

He was what they call a sceptic
    And he loved to sit and weave
High-flowing words together
    Telling what he didn't believe.

One day when we all were waiting
    For a "flood" we sat around
Smoking "nigger-head" tobacco
    And hearing Bob expound.

Hell, he said, was all a humbug,
    And he showed as clear as day
That the Bible was a fable
    And we allowed it looked that way.

"Miracles," he said, "and such like,
    Are too rank for me to stand,
As for Him they call the Saviour
    He was just a common man."

"You're a liar," someone shouted,
    "And you've got to take that back."
We all started with amazement,
    'Twas the voice of Silver Jack.

And he cracked his fists together
    And he shucked his coat and cried:
"It was in that thar religion
    My old Mother lived and died.

And although I haven't always
    Used the lord exactly right,
When I hear a chump abuse Him
    He must eat his words or fight."

Now this Bob, he warn't no coward,
    And he answered, bold and free,

"Stack your duds and cut your capers
    For there ain't no flies on me."

Well, they fought for forty minutes
    And the boys would whoop and cheer
When Jack spit up a tooth or two
    Or Bobby lost an ear.

But at last Jack got him under
    And he slugged him once or twice
And Bob straightway acknowledged
    The Divinity of Christ.

But Jack kept reasoning with him
    Till the poor cuss gave a yell
And allowed he'd been mistaken
    In his views concerning hell.

So the fierce discussion ended
    And they got up from the ground,
Then someone fetched a bottle out
    And kindly passed it 'round.

And we drank to Jack's religion
    In a solemn sort of way
And the spread of infidelity
    Was checked in camp that day.

Part II

Nature, A Witness to Religion

The empty expanses of the western landscape and the vastness of celestial regions as seen from the prairies at night invite solitary beings to reflect upon the abode of the eternal spirit and the nature of life in the hereafter. Despite its many challenges, perhaps because of them, nature is good, God is provident, and the better part of a Westerner's earthly experience will be re-enacted on an idealized plane beyond death. In some texts these manifestations of a popular Neo-Platonism are offered as a mere deistic metaphor, sometimes as literal Christian fundamentalism. This spectrum—which is at the very roots of our pluralistic society—even manifests itself in different stanzas of the same song. The situation is not unlike the spectrum of poetic mood encountered between Gray's "Elegy written in a Country Churchyard" and Blake's "The Tiger." It suggests that the kind of verse we are dealing with here might serve as a vehicle to bring great poetic themes to the people, and to implant the moods of the folk in the minds of poets greater than those who created these texts.

No. 8. *Cowboy's Call to Prayer*

Wordsworth's transcendental mood, if not his artistry, is found in this simple evocation of God's presence on the western prairies at night-fall. We do not know the author. (Hendren 68.)

> No one accused me of being good
>   No cowboy is a white washed saint
> But just last night out where the yucca stood
>   I tho't of what I should have been and ain't.
>
> The yucca looked like a parson saying prayers
>   Before I knew it I had bowed my head
> The good Lord must have put the yuccas there
>   Because He had no sky pilot instead.
>
> They point right at heaven and it seemed
>   That God was close there in the dim star light
> If I could be just like mother prayed I'd be
>   Before I mixed up wrong with right.

No. 9. *Grand Roundup*

Sleeping beneath stars has evoked the lyrical spirit of poets great and small since the days of the troubadours. When the cattle are bedded down and there is respite from rugged hours in the saddle, the solitude of the ranges gives the cowboy moments of rare communion with infinity. But at dawn the flashing eyes of his mount will call him back to the life of brawn and daring.

This is a classic among cowboy songs and hence has many variants. The same basic ideas and the same melodies ("My Bonnie" and "The Sweet Bye-and-Bye") re-appear in "The Last Roundup," greatest of the cowboy hymns and No. 29 of this collection. We give "Grand Roundup" here in two of its best poetic forms, along with three typical melodies. (Text A: PNFQ 75. Text B: JL 36. Melody A: FAC I 169, sung by Robert E. Voris, Arizona. Melody B: FAC I 501, from Edith Fowke Collection, Canada. Melody C: FAC I 504, sung by Kathy Dagel, Kansas.)

Text A. *The Grand Roundup*

Last night as I lay on the prairie,
    On a saddle I pillowed my head,
And up at the stars I lay gazing
    From out of my cool, grassy bed.
And often, and often, I wonder,
    When lying at night all alone,
If every bright star twinkling yonder
    Is a great peopled world like our own.

Chorus:

They say there's to be a grand roundup,
    And cowboys, like cattle, will stand,
To be "cut out" by the Riders of Judgment,
    Who are posted and know every brand.

Are there ranges and riders and ranches,
    Do they ring with the roughrider's refrain?
Do the cowboys e'er scrap with Comanches
    And other red men of the plain?
Do they list to the wolves in the canyon,
    Do they watch the nightbird in its flight,

SONGS—NATURE, A WITNESS TO RELIGION

Melody A. *The Cowboy's Dream*

Last night as I lay on the prai - rie,

Look-ing up to the stars in the sky, —— I

won - dered if ev - er a cow - boy —— Would

get to that sweet bye and bye. —— Oh,

yes, there will be a great round - up —— Where ——

cow - boys like cat - tle will stand, —— To be

"cut" by the Rid - er of Judg - ment, —— Who is

post - ed and knows ev - er - y brand. ——

Bring back, bring back, Oh, bring back my cow - boy to

me. —————— Bring back, bring

back, Oh, bring back my cow - boy to me. ——

Melody B.   *The Great Roundup*

At mid-night when the cat-tle are sleep-ing

—— On my sad-dle I pil-low my head, —— I

look at the heav-ens while peep-ing —— From

out of my cold, gras-sy bed. —— And

of-ten and of-ten I won-der At night while

ly-ing a-lone If ev-ery bright star —— up

yon-der —— Is a big peo-pled world like our own.

Their horses as their only companion,
    While guarding their herds thru the night?

Are the hills covered over with cattle
    In that mystic land, far, far away?
Do the ranch houses ring with the prattle
    Of dear little children at play?
And I wonder if ever I'll meet her,
    That mother the Lord took away,
And if, up in heaven, I'll greet her
    In the "roundup" that great judgment day.

Melody C. *Cowboy's Meditation*

At mid - night when the cat - tle are sleep - ing

On my sad - dle I pil - low my head, ——— And

up at the heav - ens lie peep - ing ——————— from

out of my cold, grass - y bed . ——————— And it's

of - ten and of - ten I've won - dered ——— At

night while ly - ing a - lone, ——— If

each ti - ny star way up yon - der ——— Is a

great peo - pled world like our own ———

In the east the great daylight is breaking,
    As into the saddle I spring,
The cattle from sleep are awak'ning,
    The heavenly throng taken wing.
The eyes of the broncho are flashing,
    Impatient, he pulls at the reins;
As off round the herd I go dashing,
    A reckless cowboy of the plains.

Text B.   *The Cowboy's Meditation*

When the cattle at midnight are sleeping
   On my saddle I pillow my head
And up at the stars I lie peeping
   From out of my cold grassy bed.

Often and' often I wonder
   While lying at night all alone
If every bright star gleaming yonder
   Is a big peopled world like our own.

Are there worlds with their ranges and ranches
   Do they ring with rough riders' refrains
Do the cowboys there scrap with Comanches
   And other red men of the plains?

Are the hills covered over with cattle
   In those mystic worlds far, far away,
Do the ranch houses ring with the prattle
   Of sweet little children at play?

At night in those bright stars up yonder
   Do cowboys lie down to their rest
And look at this old world and wonder
   If rough riders dash over its breast?

Do they listen to the wolves in the canyons
   Do they watch the night hawk on its flight
With their horses their only companions
   While guarding the herd through the night?

Sometimes when a bright star is twinkling
   Like a large diamond set in the sky
I find myself lying and thinking
   It may be God's Heaven on high.

I wonder if there I will meet her
   That mother the Lord took away
If in that star heaven I'll greet her
   At the round-up upon the last day.

In the east the gray twilight is breaking
And into my saddle I spring
The cattle from sleep are a-wakening
The heaven that from me takes wing.

The eyes of my bronco are flashing
Impatient he pulls at the rains
And off round the herd I go dashing,
A reckless cowboy of the plains.

No. 10. *Cowboy's Nightherd Thoughts*

A sinewed, sweat-scented outdoor life left little room for meditation. Perhaps reverie, when it was possible, became thereby all the
more meaningful, as is the case here where a vision of ultimate reality
bursts forth in the cowboy's mind like a revelation. The poem is
ascribed to Worland Grit. (WPA Writers Project, Wyoming: Library
of Congress, Document 12272, 1938-39.)

As fer wildness 'mong us cowboys
I am going to confess
That we're seldom caught a-nosin'
'Long the trail of righteousness.

And when all hunched up together,
In the roundup o'er the drive
We are apt to demonstrate it
That we're pretty much alive.

But there's times that any rider
Gets a feelin' mighty queer,
Something seems to knock his wildness
Completely out of gear.

That is when he's out on nightherd,
When the stars is twinkling dim,
And he knows there ain't nobody
On the ground but God and him.

That's the time a fellow's conscience
Hits the trail for its worth,

Gets to thinkin' he's the meanest
Bunch of wickedness on earth.

And his better innary nature
Gets a critter in ahead,
Oh, the devil's spirit in him
And I'll tell you on the dead

That he's apt to get uneasy
And a thinkin' what he'll say
For to square it with the Foreman
On the final roundup day.

Fills his head with pious notions
From the bottom to the brim
When he knows there ain't nobody
In the crowd but God and him.

No. 11. *The Range Rider's Soliloquy*

Night herding provided a natural setting for meditation, assuming there was no exciting event to rouse the cattle from their grounds and set them off on a wild stampede. In this song, which evokes images and moods like those of the *alba* or dawn songs of mediaeval troubadours, the range poet constructs the hereafter as an idealized form of life on the cattle range: Neo-Platonism of the folk, no less! (E. A. Brininstool, *Trail Dust of a Maverick,* New York: Dodd, Mead and Co., 1914, pp. 22-23.)

Sometimes when on night-herd I'm ridin',
And the stars are a-gleam in the sky,
Like millions of wee, little candles,
That twinkle and sparkle on high,
I wonder, if up there above 'em,
Are streets that are shinin' with gold,
And if it's as pretty a country
As all the sky-pilots have told?

I wonder if there are wide ranges,
And rivers and streams that's as clear,
And plains that's as blossomed with beauty
As them that I ride over here?

I wonder if summertime breezes
    Up there are like zephyrs that blow
And croon in a cadence of sweetness
    And harmony down here below?

I wonder if there, Over Yonder,
    It's true that they's never no night,
But all of the hours are sunny
    And balmy and pleasant and bright?
I wonder if birds are a-singin'
    As sweetly through all the long day
As them that I hear on the mesa
    As I go a-lopin' away?

And sometimes I wonder and wonder
    If over that lone Great Divide
I'll meet with the boys who have journeyed
    Across to the dim Farther Side?
If out on them great starry ranges
    Some day in the future, I, too,
Shall ride on a heavenly bronco
    When earth's final round-up is through?

They tell us no storms nor no blizzards
    Blow over that bloom-spangled range;
That always and ever it's summer—
    A land where there's never a change;
And nights when I lie in my blankets,
    And the star-world casts o'er me a spell,
I seem to look through on the glories
    That lie in that great Home Corral.

No. 12. *I'll Remember You Love in My Prayers*

Although this lyrical song precedes the cowboy era it was a favorite among those sung on the open ranges, and has been adapted to this new environment. Already God is but a celestialized man, and heaven a celestialized replica of life on earth. Add the vistas of ranges, the cowboys with their toil and gear, and the "western" metaphor for ultimate reality will have been formulated. (Text: *The Family Guide Songster* [c. 1875], Vol. II, p. 8. Melody: Victor 21289, Teneva Ramblers.)

When the curtains of night are pinned back by the stars
    And the beautiful moon sweeps the skies
And the dewdrops of heaven are kissing the rose
    It is then that my memory flies,
As if on the wings of some beautiful dove
    In haste with the message it bears
To bring you a kiss of affection and say
    "I remember you, love, in my prayers."

    Go where you will on land or at sea
      I'll share all your sorrows and cares
    And at night when I kneel by my bedside to pray
      I'll remember you, love, in my prayers.

I have loved you too fondly to ever forget
    The love you have spoken for me,
The kiss of affection still worn on my lips
    When you told me how true you would be.
I know not if fortune be fickle or friend
    Or if time or your memory wears,
I know that I love you wherever you roam,
    And remember you, love, in my prayers.

When heavenly angels are guarding the good
    As God has ordained them to do
In answer to prayers I have offered to him
    I know there is one watching you.
And may its bright spirit be with you through life
    To guide you up heaven's bright stairs
And meet with one who has loved you so true
    And remembers you, love, in her prayers.

I'll Remember You Love in My Prayers

When the cur - tains of night are pinned back by the
stars And the beau - ti - ful moon sweeps the skies, ——
—— And the dew - drops of heav - en are kiss - ing the
rose, It is then that my mem - o - ry flies, ——
—— As —— if on the wings of some beau - ti - ful
dove, In —— haste with the mes - sage it bears, ——
—— To —— bring you a kiss of af - fec - tion and
say, "I re - mem - ber you, love, in my prayers." ——

Part III

Death on the Range

Cowboy songs, like the folk songs of the whole Christian world, are permeated with the topic of death: death looked upon generally as a passage of the imperishable soul into an idealized existence in the presence of God, and reunited with next of kin. These songs have a homiletic quality in which life is seen not as an end in itself but as a preparation for the hereafter. "Western" qualities in these songs consist of images of the western landscape (the wind-swept grass-covered lone prairie, coyotes, buffalo, buzzards, rattlesnakes), the cowboy's work routine (range riding, cutting, roping and branding, trail driving, night herding, trail's end carousal), and the moral commitments which best prepare him for the Last Ride (faithfulness to wife, mother, and family; forthrightness, masculine vigor, guilelessness, candor, even violence). The homiletic content of texts in this section presents a wide spectrum from austere Puritanism (Nos. 16 and 20), to the simplest trust in the all-encompassing goodness of God (Nos. 13, 18, 19).

No. 13. *The Dying Cowboy*

Death is a pervasive subject in cowboy songs (as indeed it is in all lyrical forms of expression), and "The Dying Cowboy" is the best known and most loved song about it. There are hundreds of texts, variants so numerous that it nears the proportions of an epic poem. Space will not permit us, in this document, to trace its history from "The Ocean Burial" to its emergence as one of the greatest folk songs produced on this continent.

Despite his wish to be buried back east and among his own kin, circumstances force the cowboys to bury their comrade on the lone prairie whose characteristic vistas, carefully particularized in the song, form a violent contrast with the gentler scenes of the cowboy's youth.

We have purposely chosen one of the longest texts in order to reveal as much as possible the western tags imbedded in the song, which has often served as a hymn (J. Frank Dobie in interview with Fifes, FAC I 549, p. 2. Ben Moore, Sr., *Butterfield Seven Years With The Wild Indians,* O'Donnell, Texas, 1945, p. 33). (Text: *Hobo News,*

Vol. 8. Melody A: Library of Congress #2621B, recorded by John A. Lomax, Melody B: FAC I 178, John Donald Robb Collection, New Mexico.)

Melody A. *The Dying Cowboy*

Oh, bury me not on the lone prairie,
These words came low and mournfully
From the pallid lips of a youth who lay
On his dying bed at the close of day.

He had wasted and pined till on his brow
Death's shades were slowly gathering now;
He thought of his home and his loved ones nigh,
As the cowboys gathered to see him die.

Melody B. *The Dying Cowboy*

"Oh, bur - y me not — — on the lone prai - rie," — These words came slow — and mourn - ful - ly, — From the pal - lid lips — of a youth who lay, — On his cold damp bed — at the close of day. —

"Oh, bury me not on the lone prairie
Where the wild coyotes will howl o'er me,
Where the west wind sweeps and the grasses wave,
And sunbeams rest on the prairie grave.

"In fancy I listen to the well-known words
Of the free wild winds and the song of the birds;
I think of home and the cottage in the bower
And the scenes I loved in my childhood's hour.

"It matters not, I've often been told,
Where the body lies when the heart grows cold.
Yet grant, oh, grant this wish to me:
Oh, bury me not on the lone prairie.

"Then bury me not on the lone prairie
In a narrow grave six by three,
Where the buffalo paws o'er a prairie sea,
Oh, bury me not on the lone prairie.

"I've always wished to be laid, when I died,
In the little churchyard on the green hillside;
By my father's grave, there let mine be,
Oh, bury me not on the lone prairie.

"O'er me then a mother's prayer
And a sister's tears might mingle there,
Where my friends can come and weep o'er me;
Oh, bury me not on the lone prairie.

"Oh, bury me not on the lone prairie,
In a narrow grave just six by three
Where the buzzard waits and the wind blows free,
Oh, bury me not on the lone prairie.

"There is another whose tears may be shed
For one who lies on a prairie bed.
It pained me then, and it pains me now—
She has curled these locks, she has kissed this brow.

"Oh, why did I roam o'er the wild prairie?
She's waiting there at home for me,
But her lovely face ne'er more I'll see.
Oh, bury me not on the lone prairie.

"These locks she has curled, shall the rattlesnake kiss?
This brow she has kissed, shall the cold grave press?
For the sake of her who will weep for me,
Oh, bury me not on the lone prairie.

"Oh, bury me not on the lone prairie,
Where the wild coyotes will howl o'er me,
Where the buzzard beats, and the wind goes free.
Oh, bury me not on the lone prairie.

"Oh, bury me not," and his voice failed there.
But we took no heed of his dying prayer,
In a narrow grave just six by three,
We buried him there on the lone prairie.

Yes, we buried him there on the lone prairie
Where the owl all night hoots mournfully;
And the blizzard beats and the wind blows free
O'er his lonely grave on the lone prairie.

May the light-winged butterfly pause to rest
O'er him who sleeps on the prairie's crest;
May the Texas rose in the breezes wave
O'er him who sleeps in the prairie's grave.

Where the dewdrops glow and the butterflies rest,
And the flowers bloom o'er the prairie's crest;
Where the wild coyote and the wind sports free
On a wet saddle blanket lay a cowboy-ee.

"Oh, bury me not on the lone prairie,
Where the wild coyotes will howl o'er me,
Where the rattlesnakes hiss and the crow flies free,
Oh, bury me not on the lone prairie."

Oh, we buried him there on the lone prairie,
Where the wild rose blooms and the wind blows free.
Oh his young face ne'er more to see,
For we buried him there on the lone prairie.

And the cowboys now, as they roam the plain—
For they marked the spot where his bones were lain—
Fling a handful of roses o'er his grave,
With a prayer to God his soul to save.

"Oh, bury me not on the lone prairie,
Where the wolves can howl and growl o'er me,
Fling a handful of roses o'er my grave
With a prayer to Him who my soul will save."

No. 14. *The Glory Trail*

The classic triangular love theme of fiction plays second fiddle
to the metaphysical conflict of man torn between the quest for ultimate
reality and humdrum existence. "Hitching your wagon to a star" is as
nothing compared to the top-hand of the Lazy-J ranch who threw his
lasso on a mountain lion. Cowboy metaphor rings true throughout.
(Text: Charles Badger Clark, *Sun and Saddle Leather*, Boston: R. G.

Badger, 1915, pp. 39-41. Melody: B. A. Botkin, *A Treasury of Western Folklore,* New York: Crown Publishers, 1951, p. 765.)

Away High Up in the Mogliones

Way high up in the Mogollons among the mountain tops
A lion cleaned a yearling's bones and licked his thankful chops,
When on the picture who should ride, a trippin' down a slope
But High Chinned Bob with sinful pride and maverick-hungry rope.

> "Oh, glory be to me," says he, "and fame's unfadin' flowers,
> All meddlin' hands are far away,
> I ride my good top hoss today,
> And I'm top rope of the Lazy J.
> Hi, kitty cat, you're ours!"

That lion licked his paw so brown and dreamed soft dreams of veal,
And then the circling loop swung down and roped him round his meal.
He yowled quick fury to the world 'til all the hills yelled back,
The top hoss gave a snort and whirled and Bob caught up the slack.

    "Oh, glory be to me," says he, "I hit the glory trail,
        No human man as I have read
        Darst loop a ragin' lion's head,
        Nor ever hoss could drag one dead
    Until we told the tale."

Way high up on the Mogollons that top hoss done his best
Through whippin' brush and rattlin' stones from canyon floor to crest,
But ever when Bob turned and hoped a limp remains to find
A red-eyed lion, belly roped but healthy, loped behind.

    "Oh, glory be to me," grunts he, "this Glory Trail is rough,
        Yet even 'til the Judgment Morn
        I'll keep the dally round the horn
        For never any hero born
    Could stoop to holler 'nuff."

Three suns had rode their circle home beyond the desert's rim
And turned their star herds loose to roam the ranges high and dim,
Yet up and down and round and 'cross Bob pounded weak and wan,
For pride still glued him to his hoss and glory drove him on.

    "Oh, glory be to me," sighs he, "he kaint be drug to death,
        But now I know beyond a doubt
        Them heros I have read about
        Was only fools that stuck it out
    To end of mortal breath."

Way high up in the Mogollons a prospect man did swear
That moon dreams melted down his bones and hoisted up his hair,
A ribby cow hoss thundered by, a lion trailed along,
A rider, gaunt but chin on high, yelled out a crazy song:

    "Oh, glory be to me," cries he, "and to my noble noose,
        Oh, stranger, tell my pard below—
        I took a rampin' dream in tow,
        And if I never lay him low
    I'll never turn him loose!"

No. 15. *Over the Trail*

The poem has the setting, the mood, and even the dominant ana-
pestic rhythms of an elegy. But images, metaphors, and setting are
true to the new environment, to the cowboy idiom, and the deliberate
tempo of the range. (WPA Writers Project, New Mexico: Library of
Congress, Document W 1026, 1936-37.)

> Out on the desert sear and brown,
>> Under the edge of a western sky,
> A trail leads forth from a 'doby town,
>> To the resting place of those that die.
>
> A group of mounds in a dreary waste,
>> A cluster of graves in a desolate land,
> Where rich and poor alike are placed
>> Under the desert's drifting sand.
>
> Saint and sinner and youth and maid,
>> Gringo and greaser and peon slave,
> Lie side by side, neath the cactus shade,
>> In sodless, flowerless, lonely grave.
>
> Somebody's darling or somebody's friend,
>> Under each wooden cross there lies,
> Someone's life drama played to the end,
>> To selfish mortals' censuring eyes.
>
> Joy and sorrow, smiles and tears,
>> Hopes that perish and friends that fail,
> These they have known in the vanished years,
>> Ere their last sad journey over the trail.
>
> Toil and trouble or sin and shame
>> Have clouded the light of their lives now past,
> In the long hard struggle for wealth and fame;
>> Then death and shroud and the grave at last.
>
> The autumn sunset paints the west,
>> The gates of the great corral swing wide,
> And the long nights fall on their endless rest,
>> By the trail that crosses the Great Divide.

No. 16. *The Cowboy's Lament*

This song vies with "The Dying Cowboy" (No. 13) for honors as the most printed, most sung, and most varied of all cowboy songs. Because of its dependence on notorious British predecessors ("The Unfortunate Rake," "Old Rosin the Beau," etc.) it has demanded more attention from ballad critics than any other cowboy song. (See: Wayland D. Hand, "Wo sind die Strassen von Laredo"? Die Entwincklungsgeschichte einer amerikanischen Cowboy Ballade. *Festschrift für Will-Erich Peuckert zum 60. Geburtstag dargebracht von Freunden und Schülern,* Berlin, 1955, pp. 144-161. Phillips Barry, "Some Aspects of Folk-Song," *Journal of American Folklore,* XXV [1912], p. 277. N. Howard Thorp and Austin and Alta Fife, *Songs of the Cowboys,* New York: Clarkson N. Potter, 1966, pp. 148-190. Commercial recording: Kenneth Goldstein, "The Unfortunate Rake": Folkways FS 3805.)

The song is the plaint of a cowboy who, about to die from a gunshot wound, unburdens his conscience of a sinful life, urges men of his kind to avoid the obvious pitfalls (women, cards, alcohol, violence), begs for a humane burial. Like sagebrush on western ranges, the song has proliferated in the minds of singers and thus achieved epic proportions. We are concerned here with its uses as a hymn and its interest as a vehicle for religious and transcendental expressions in the cowboy mode. One integral text with music is given, and a composite text made up of stanzas pertaining to the subject of this monograph, wherever encountered. Note that there is a stanza from a Swedish version, which came from Minnesota. (Text: Sharlot M. Hall, "Songs of the Old Cattle Trails," *Out West,* March 1908, p. 217. Melody: Myra E. Hull, "Cowboy Ballads," *The Kansas Historical Quarterly* [Feb. 1939], VIII, No. 1, p. 50.)

> As I rode out to Latern in Barin
> As I rode out so early one day,
> 'Twas there I espied a handsome young cowboy
> All dressed in white linen and clothes for the grave.
>
> Then play your fife lowly and beat your drum slowly,
> And play the Dead March as you bear me along;
> Take me to the graveyard and lay the sod o'er me,
> I am a poor cowboy and I know I've done wrong.

The Cowboy's Lament

'Twas once in my sad - dle I used to be
hap - py, 'Twas once in my sad - dle I
used to be gay; But I first took to
drink - ing, then to gam - bling, A
shot from a six - shoot - er took my life a - way.

'Twas once in the saddle I used to go dashing,
   'Twas once in the saddle I used to be gay;
But I first took to drinking and then to card playing,
    Got shot in a fight, and now I must die.

Go gather around you a crowd of young cowboys,
   And tell them the story of this my sad fate;
And tell them to stop all their gambling and drinking,
    And all their wild ways before it's too late.

Go write a letter to my gray-headed mother,
   And break the news gently to my sisters so dear;
And then there's another dearer far than a mother,
    Who'll bitterly weep when she knows I am here.

Go bring me a cup of pure cold water,
   A cup of cold water, the poor fellow said;
But when I returned, the spirit had departed,
    And gone to the Giver—the cowboy was dead.

Composite text:

O, beat the drum loudly and play the fife proudly
    And scare the devil off as you carry me along
Then chase him o'er the hillside and beat him o'er the meadow
    For I'm a poor cowboy and know I've done wrong.
          *   *   *

When the liberated soul from the earthly bond
    Has swung itself up to the eternal land
Then hide me in the mound out there on the hill—
    A cowboy who died at the murderer's hand.
          *   *   *

My home and my relation I left them in Boston,
    My parents knew not where their poor son had gone,
I first came to Texas and hired to a ranchman,
    Now hell is my doom for I know I've done wrong.
          *   *   *

Go send for the minister to cry and pray o'er me
    Go send for a doctor to cure me or try
Go send for that pretty girl who's the cause of my ruin
    So that I can forgive her before I must die.
          *   *   *

"Men der är en annan, mer dyr an en moder,
    O, bringa en helsning till henne, min vän;
Sag, att hon ej grater, ty vi skola ater
    En gang bortom dödsfloden mötas igen.
          *   *   *

"O gather around you a crowd of gay cowboys,
    And tell them the story of a comrade's sad fate,
Give each one and all of them timely good warning
    To mend their wild rovings before it's too late."
          *   *   *

Go bring to my bedside a class of bold rangers
    Who shoot fast and straight
And give them a warning to stop the gold gambling
    To stop the gold gambling before it's too late.
          *   *   *

"Please gather up my last hand of poker
    The one that I dropped when I got my death wound
Send it and my six gun home to my brother
    After you've buried me deep in the tomb.

"Tell him these things are what ruined his brother
    And never to part with the last fatal hand

But carry it always just as a reminder
    If e'er he should drift to this wild cattle land."
            *   *   *

Once in my saddle I used to go dashing
    Once in my saddle I used to go gay
But now I've took drinking then card playing
    God shorten my breath for I am dying to day.
            *   *   *

I've missed life eternal, I'm bound for destruction
    But God was willing that I should do so
Grieve not while thinking of my condition
    I'm a vile sinner, and now I must go.
            *   *   *

Get four wild cowboys to carry my body
    And two little girls to follow along
A golden trumpet to sound in the morning
    To let my friends know that I am gone.
            *   *   *

Go bring me a cup of pure cold water,
    A cup of cold water, the poor fellow said;
But when I returned, the spirit had departed,
    And gone to the Giver—the cowboy was dead.
            *   *   *

"Go bring me a glass of cold water
    To cool my hot temples," this cowboy he said,
But when I had returned he had gone to his Giver
    This once handsome cowboy lay senseless and dead.

No. 17. *Texas Cowboy*

The moods and rhythms of night herding songs lent themselves to reverie and contemplation about death and immortality. Here interest is on the cowboy's Last Ride and the one credential he has for salvation: that he "sometimes acted like a man." (Text: JL 458, Melody: Gasper Bolivar, Archive of Folk and Primitive Music, Indiana University, 359.5.)

I'm going to leave old Texas now
They have no room for the longhorn cow
They've plowed and fenced my cattle range
And the people there are all so strange.

I'll take my horse, I'll take my rope
And strike the trail upon a lope

The Cowman's Lament

I'm going to leave —— old Tex - as now —— They have no room for the long-horn cow —— They've plowed and fenced —— My cat - tle range —— And the peop - le there —— are all so strange —— I'll take my horse —— I'll take my rope —— And strike the trail —— up - on a lope —— say a - di - os —— to the Al - a - mo —— And turn my face —— towards Mex - i - co.

I'll bid *adios* to the Alamo
And turn my face towards Mexico.

I'll spend my days on the wide, wide range
For the people there are not so strange
The hard, hard ground will be my bed
And the saddle seat will hold my head.

And when I awaken from my dreams
I'll eat my bread and my sardines
And when my ride on earth is done
I'll take my turn with the Holy One.

I'll tell St. Peter that I know
A cowboy's soul ain't white as snow
Yet in that far off cattle land
He sometimes acted like a man.

[Refrain as sung by Frank Goodwyn, FAC I 247:]

Whoa, dogies, whoa-oh
Whoa-ooh, oooh.
The people there are all so strange.

[Variants of last line of refrain:]

I'll turn my face toward Mexico.

A saddle seat will hold my head.

I'll take my turn with the Holy One.

No. 18. *The Cowboy's Faith*

The bland simplicity of this statement about a cowboy's hopes for
the life after death—his pony to ride and the night sounds of the range
—evokes an image like that of the mediaeval minstrel of Notre Dame
who danced and juggled for the Virgin, these being the only talents he
could muster for her service. (Hendren 462.)

What's that, sir, no horses in heaven you say!
Hold on, Mr. Preacher, don't talk that way,
Don't call it a country of pleasures and rest
For us sun-dried punchers out here in the west,
Unless there's some horses across the Divide
That we can lasso and pal with and ride.

We don't want no wings, or a harp, don't you see,
We want to live on in a land that is free,
Where western ain't thick [sic] and the fences are few
And all honest cowboys have something to do.

— 49 —

We want just a blanket out under the sky
Where we can count stars and the clouds floating by,
We want the night song of the cricket and owl,
We want to get lonesome when coyotes howl.

I'll pine there in Heaven if pinto ain't there,
To leave him behind, sir, to me won't look square,
Us two have been pardners for seven long years
A ridin' on circle and trailin' the steers.

So when I checks in and lay down my rope
I ain't got much gospel, but this is my hope,
I'll step through the darkness along trails that's strange
And find pinto waitin' up there on the range.

No. 19.　*Crossing the Divide*

　　We agree with N. Howard Thorp that this is "one of the best of
the lot." Range experiences and familiar objects in the cowboy's life
are vested with metaphorical richness to evoke the Christian life, salvation, and life in the hereafter. The idiom of the range is used without
apology, and its virility and candor remind us that eloquence and
elocution do not go hand-in-hand. (N. Howard Thorp, *Songs of the
Cowboys,* Boston and New York: Houghton Mifflin Co., 1921, pp.
55-56. Ascribed to J. W. Foley.)

Parson, I'm a maverick, just runnin' loose an' grazin',
　　Eatin' where's th' greenest grass an' drinkin' where I choose;
Had to rustle in my youth an' never had no raisin';
　　Wasn't never halter broke an' I ain't much to lose;
Used to sleepin' in a bag an' livin' in a slicker;
　　Church folks never branded me—I don't know as they tried;
Wish you'd say a prayer for me an' try to make a dicker
　　For the best they'll give me when I cross the Big Divide.

Tell 'em I ain't corralled a night in more'n twenty;
　　Tell 'em I'm rawboned an' rough an' ain't much for looks;
Tell 'em I don't need much grief because I've had a-plenty;
　　I don't know how bad I am 'cause I ain't kept no books.
Tell 'em I'm a maverick a-runnin' loose unbranded;
　　Tell 'em I shoot straight an' quick an' ain't got much to hide;

Have 'em come an' size me up as soon as I get landed,
    For the best they'll give me when I cross the Great Divide.

Tell 'em I rode straight an' square an' never grabbed for leather;
    Never roped a crippled steer or rode a sore-backed horse;
Tell 'em I've bucked wind an' rain an' every sort of weather,
    Had my tilts with A. K. Hall an' Captain R. E. Morse.
Don't hide nothin' from 'em, whether it be sweet or bitter,
    Tell 'em I'll stay on th' range, but if I'm shut outside
I'll abide it like a man because I ain't no quitter;
    I ain't going to change just when I cross th' Big Divide.

Tell 'em, when th' Roundup comes for all us human critters,
    Just corral me with my kind an' run a brand on me;
I don't want to be corralled with hypocrites an' quitters;
    Brand me just for what I am—an' I'm just what you see.
I don't want no steam-het stall or bran-mash for my ration;
    I just want to meet th' boss an' face him honest-eyed,
Show him just what chips I got an' shove 'em in for cashin';
    That's what you can tell 'em when I cross the Big Divide.

No. 20. *Gambling on the Sabbath*

There is a cluster of twenty or more ballads, with innumerable variants and interlocking texts, dealing with the complete moral decay of a young man who leaves home for a life of violence and sensuality in the West, and who ends up confessing his evil ways when he is about to be executed. Antecedents to these songs existed in the ballad tradition of Great Britain before the mass movements of Anglo-Americans into the plains states and beyond. It is important to note the sharp contrast in the moral content of this song and "Crossing the Divide," No. 19. The West has indeed had a pluralistic culture from the first decade of its colonization. Two texts are given to suggest the vegetative transformations through which the song has passed. (Text A: Hendren 879. Text B: Hendren 329. Melody: B. A. Botkin, *A Treasury of Western Folklore,* New York: Crown Publishers, 1951, p. 778.)

Text A.

A poor misguided boy did dare,
To disregard his father's care;
He would not heed his sister's tears,
And would not hear his mother's prayer.

From all advice he turned away,
And cards and dice he learned to play,
At last a comrade he did slay,
While gambling on the Sabbath Day.

Oh, who could tell the mother's thought,
When first to her the news was brought?
The Sheriff said her son was sought,
And into prison he was brought.
His father, sixty years of age,
The best of counsel did engage,
To see if something could be done,
To save his disobedient son.

Nothing could the attorneys do,
The testimony was too true,
That he, the fatal weapon drew,
And pierced his comrade's body through.
His poor old mother, sitting by,
She heard them tell the reason why,
Her son in prison had to lie
Till on the gallows he would die.

Oh, hear him on the gallows tell,
His weeping parents fare-thee-well;
"My soul now feels in mental hell,
And soon with demons I must dwell.
Dearest sister, do not weep
For soon with demons I must sleep,
My soul, alas! I cast away,
While gambling on the Sabbath Day.

"Oh, gray-haired mother, now good-bye,
In one short hour I must die;
From your advice I strayed, oh my—
It breaks my heart to see you cry.
Come, wife, and lay your head down here,
And let me feel your falling tear,
The cruel man will take my life,
Take me from my darling wife.

"But I leave with you one precious joy,
And that is our own darling boy.

Oh, teach him wisely what to do,
How to love and care for you
And from your side to never stray
While I am molding back to clay.

"Oh, teach him to remember me,
Wher'er on earth that he might be,
And every night to kneel and pray,
That we may meet in Heaven some day.
And let the last of things be this:
To take from you a farewell kiss,
The time has come for me to die,
It breaks my heart to see you cry."

The Sheriff cut the slender cord,
His soul must go to meet his Lord;
The Doctor said, "The boy is dead,"
And from the earth his spirit fled.
The weeping mother cried aloud:
"Pray God to save this gazing crowd,
That they may never be cast away,
For gambling on the Sabbath Day."

Gambling on the Sabbath Day

A poor un - worth - y son who —— dared
To dis. - re - gard a fa - ther's care
Or lis - ten —— to a moth - er's prayer
While gam - bling on the Sab - bath day.

Text B.

"Now come, young man, and listen to me,
A sad and mournful history
And may you never forgetful be
Of what I tell this day to thee.

"Oh! I was thoughtless, young, and gay
And often broke the Sabbath Day.
In wickedness I took delight,
And sometimes done what wasn't right.

"Oh, who could tell a mother's thought
When first the news to her was brought.
The sheriff said her son was sought
And into prison must be brought.

"My father, sixty years of age,
The best of counsel did engage
To see if something could be done
To save his disobedient son.

"Only a mother standing by
To hear them tell the reason why
Her son in prison he must lie
Till on the scaffold he must die.

"So farewell, Mother, do not weep,
Though soon with demons I will sleep.
My soul now feels its mental hell
And soon with demons I will dwell."

The sheriff cut the tender cord,
His soul went up to meet its Lord.
The doctor said, "The wretch is dead,
His spirit from his body fled."

His weeping mother cried aloud,
"Oh God, do save this gazing crowd,
That none may ever have to pay
For gambling on the Sabbath Day."

No. 21.   *Good-bye to the Plains*

A cowboy takes leave of earthly friends and environment in antici-
pation of death: pals, danger, anguish; pony, cattle, gear; dawn, family,
sweetheart. He is riding into eternity. (Text and melody: Decca 5532,
sung by the Carter Family.)

Good-bye to the Plains

Good - bye to the pals of the prai - rie, ——
—— Good - bye to the pals of the plain, ——
—— Good - bye to the dash and the dan - ger, ——
—— Good - bye to the heart - aches and pain.

Good-bye to the pals of the prairie,
    Good-bye to the pals of the plain,
Good-bye to the dash and the danger,
    Good-bye to the heartaches and pain.

Good-bye to my faithful old pony,
    Take care of him, boys, when I go.
I'm riding away on life's round-up,
    Away to where the sun sinks low.

Good-bye to the lowing of cattle,
    Good-bye to the clanking of spurs,

Good-bye to the light and the shadows,
    Good-bye to the wild life and steers.

Good-bye to the dawning's first blushes
    That far in the east faintly glow,
I'm riding away on life's round-up,
    Away to where the sun sinks low.

Good-bye to the girls and the boys,
    Good-bye to all of my friends,
Good-bye to the dear girl, my sweetheart,
    For I know this is my end.

For the Trail Rider comes with His summons,
    And I'm weary and ready to go,
For I'm riding away on life's round-up,
    Away to where the sun sinks low.

No. 22.   *The Cowboy's Last Ride*

    This lament for a dying puncher echoes the spirit of "The Dying Cowboy" and of "The Grand Roundup" (Nos. 13 and 29). Dying a violent death during a cattle stampede, the cowboy prays for salvation and reunion with his deceased mother. The other riders bury him on the prairie, confident that his petition will be granted. (Hendren 974.)

Way out on the western prairie,
    At the close of a long, weary day,
The cattle had just stampeded,
    There a dying cowboy lay.
His comrades were gathered around him,
    And the range boss lifted his head,
With a voice that touched every heart that night,
    The dying cowboy said:—

"Oh! write to my dear old mother,
    Down south by the Rio Grande,
Tell her the angels are calling me,
    To the range of another land,
Just say that some day I will meet her
    At the round-up in heaven above,
Where the riders of judgment will guide us
    O'er the pastures of gladness and love."

And out on the lonely prairie,
　　There we dug out a grave in the clay,
And in earth's arms he's sleeping,
　　Just awaiting judgment day.
Awaiting the last big round-up,
　　When the cowboys like dogies will stand
To be picked by the riders of judgment,
　　To ride in another land.

Part IV

Hymns: Parodies of Cowboy Songs

In the songs of this section everything indicates the creation of revival hymns by willful parody of songs from the cowboy and western repertoire. We are confident that more such parodies would show up if we had been able to consult published collections of revival music, or to have heard first-hand over a long period renditions of camp and gospel music in their natural environment. Sacred parodies of cowboy and western songs were also recorded on 78 rpm records and broadcast by radio, especially on those networks operated by fundamentalist sects.

No. 23. Round-Up Lullaby

The best known of the night herding songs has the slow rhythms of reverence and a nocturnal setting with transcendental and spiritualistic overtones, if you make the most obvious analogy: that man is to God and eternity what the dogie is to the ranch boss. We give the song here as it was most typically sung on the ranges, plus one text to which a revivalist stanza has been added. (Text A: Hendren 338. Text B: Hendren 502. Melody: FAC I 510, sung by Kathy Dagel, Kansas.)

Text A.

Slow down, dogies, quit your roving around,
You've wandered and trampled all over the ground;
Oh, haze along dogies, feed kinda slow,
And don't be forever on the go;
    Move slow, little dogies, move slow.
    Heigh-ho, heigh-ho, heigh-ho.

I've trail-herded, cross herded, night herded too,
But to keep you together is what I can't do;
My horse is leg weary, and I'm awful tired,
But if you get away I'm sure I get fired—
    Bunch up, little dogies, bunch up.
    Heigh-ho, heigh-ho, heigh-ho.

Night Herding Song

Slow down, do - gies, quit your rov - ing a - round, You'v wan - dered and tram - pled all ov - er the ground; Oh, haze a - long do - gies, feed kind - a slow, And don't be for - ev - er on the go —— Move slow, lit - tle do - gies, move slow.

Oh say, little dogies, when you gonna lay down
And quit this forever shifting around?
My legs they are weary, my seat it is sore,
So lay down, little dogies, like you laid down before—
    Lay down, little dogies, lay down,
    Heigh-ho, heigh-ho, heigh-ho.

Lay still, little dogies, since you have laid down,
Stretch away out on the big open ground;
Snore loud, little dogies, and still the wild sound
That will go away when the day rolls around—
    Lay still, little dogies, lay still,
    Heigh-ho, heigh-ho, heigh-ho.

Text B.

Slow down, little dogies, and take your time,
Tomorrow we'll be crossing the Mexican line,
To the green pastures yonder, to the plains on high,
Slow down, little dogies, while I sing a round-up lullaby.

> Yip-ee-ki-yi; yip-ee-ki-yi,
> Some day we'll be heading on high
> And riding a new range up yonder
> To the tune of a round-up lullaby.

When our work is over and He calls us home,
We'll find new pastures and never more roam;
We'll ride a new round-up on the range in the sky,
And I'll be riding Old Paint with a round-up lullaby.

No. 24. *Soon (Home on the Range)*

"Home on the Range," since its emergence as Franklin D. Roosevelt's favorite song in the 1930's, is probably the best known and the least "cowboy" of all the cowboy songs. With sacred words it became a favorite revival hymn. (Text: JL 430, composed by Carolyn Morgan, cowgirl preacher. Melody: traditional.)

> The time is quite near for our Lord to appear
> Oh, I know the trumpet will soon blow,
> The angels will sing, and Jesus will bring
> All the ones that I love up on high.

> Soon, soon in the sky
> Oh, I know I am going by and by
> The angels will sing and Jesus will bring
> All the ones that I love up on high.

Soon

The time is quite near for our Lord to appear, Oh I know the trum-pet will blow, —— The
an - gels will sing, and Je - sus will bring All the
ones that I love up on high. ——
Soon, soon in the sky —— Oh, I
know I am going by and by. —— The
an - gels will sing and Je - sus will bring All the
ones that I love up on high. ——

No. 25. *Red River Valley*

The two hymns which follow are both derived from "Red River Valley," a favorite among cowboy songs, though it probably originated in the lumber camps of Canada. The first depends very closely on

"Red River Valley" for melody, mood, and images; the second keeps little save the melody. It stresses the expiation of original and recurrent sin in the martyrdom of Christ, and urges the sinner to seek the gift of salvation while there is yet time. (Text A: PNFQ 391. Text B: PNFQ 228, from "The Young Soldier;" the Salvation Army Sunday School paper. Melody: traditional.)

Red River Valley

From these prai - ries of life I'll be leav - ing, —

— I will go to that ranch in the sky; —

— Where the Lord is for me now pre - par - ing —

— A place where I'll live by and by.

Text A.

From these prairies of life I'll be leaving,
I will go to that ranch in the sky;
Where the Lord is for me now preparing,
A place where I'll live by and by.

Oh, consider the way you are going;
Does it lead to the ranch in the sky?
And remember the Saviour is waiting
And expecting you there by and by.

What about the life you are now living;
　　And the things that you do every day?
Don't be angry because I am asking,
　　Stop and think—will it pay, will it pay?

Just swing into the saddle for Jesus,
　　And get onto that heavenward way.
At the gate He is waiting to greet us,
　　If we live the one life that does pay.

Text B.　　*Jesus Saves From Sin*

At your heart Jesus stands, He is pleading
　　For an entrance; Oh, let Him come in!
He will bring you His pardon and comfort,
　　He will save you from all of your sin.

Can you see His dear hands with the nail prints?
　　See the wounds in His feet and His side?
Oh, list to His cry, "It is finished."
　　'Twas to save you from sin that He died.

Can you see, His blood is still flowing,
　　So freely for you and for me?
Won't you turn to Him while he's pleading?
　　He offers His mercy so free.

Then open your heart while He's waiting,
　　Lest in sorrow He turn soon away;
Soon His calling may cease, and His knocking
　　Oh! open to Him while you may.

Part V

Cowboy Hymns

The production of revival hymns by the direct parody of folk songs (and, indeed, the reverse process!) has no doubt taken place wherever and whenever cultures have existed which have discernable priestly and lay sectors. With respect to the revivalist parodies of songs popular in the American West (exclusive of cowboy songs which are treated separately) we cite the following examples: "My Story" from "The Prisoner's Song"; "Jesus Is Coming" from "Birmingham Jail"; "You Will Need Jesus" from "Nobody's Darling"; "When I Make My Last Move" from "The Dream of the Miner's Child"; "The Rich Man" and "He Has Risen" from "Floyd Collins." There is also a revivalist parody to "Red Wing." (JL 430, pp. 1, 2.)

No. 26. *Rounded Up in Glory*

This is a full-blown gospel hymn in the cowboy mode. God will assemble the faithful and protect them from adversity, just as the range boss rounds up the dogies of the prairies and drives them to the comforting shelter of the home corral. (Text: JL 316, "Dedicated to the cattlemen of Texas September 23, 1898." Melody: Capitol record 20067, Tex Ritter.)

I've been thinking today
And my thoughts began to stray
Your memory's to me worth more than gold,
As you ride upon the plain
'Mid the sunshine and the rain
You'll be rounded up within the Master's fold.

He will round us up in glory by and by
He will round us up in glory by and by
When the milling time is o'er
And we stampede no more
We'll be rounded up in glory by and by.

May we lift our voices high
Till the sweet by and by
And be known by the brand of God's love,
For His property we are
And He'll know us from afar
When He rounds us up in glory above.

As we look upon the plain
To the cowboys that have fame
While the storm and lightnin' flashes by
We will meet to part no more
Upon the golden shore
As we all round up in glory by and by.

Rounded Up in Glory

No. 27. *Star of the Western Skies*

An aura of reverence and stateliness—called by J. Frank Dobie the true tempo of the range—is achieved in this song. The image of a star leading the lonely caravan westward suggests the star of Bethlehem. (Hendren 178.)

Lonely caravan a-rollin' through the night,
Lonely caravan, you know the trail is right,
For a guiding star shines from afar,
    Leads the wagon train along.

    Star of the western skies, keep guiding me
        Over hill and dale and winding trail and over the great divide,
    Land of the western skies, abide in me,
        For on the darkest night your light shall be my guide.

Wheels a grinding as we're winding on and on
Through the night and through the coming dawn.
Star of the western skies, keep on guiding me
    Till my restless heart is satisfied.

No. 28. *Cowboy's Salvation Song*

This hymn has the active rhythms and characteristic images of a trail-driving song: roundup, cutting, trail driving, rustlers, the home ranch, branding—even the inevitable dust of the cattle drive—have metaphorical implications for man's pilgrimage to heaven. (Robert Carr, *Black Hills Ballads,* Denver: Reed Publishing Co., 1902, pp. 27-28.)

    Oh, it's move along, you dogies, don't be driftin' by th' way,
    Fer there's goin' to be a round-up an' a cuttin'-out, they say,
    Of all th' devil's dogies an' a movin' at sunrise,
    An' you'd better be preparin' fer a long drive to th' skies.

Oh, it's move along, you dogies, don't be driftin' by th' way,
Fer th' boss of all th' rus'lers is a-comin' 'round to-day.
So you'd better be a-movin', throw your dust right in his eyes,
An' hit th' trail a-flyin' fer th' home-ranch in th' skies.

So it's move along, you dogies, fer th' devil has in hand
A bunch of red-hot irons an' he's surely goin' to brand
All his dogies, an' some others, an' mighty suddin, too,
So you'd better be a-movin' so he won't be brandin' you.

So it's move along, you dogies, tho' you have th' mange o' sin,
There's a range you're sure to shake it when you come a-trailin' in,
Where th' grass is allers growin' an' th' water's allers pure,
So it's move along, you dogies, 'fore th' devil brands you sure.

No. 29. *Last Round-Up*

This is by all counts the greatest of the cowboy and western
hymns. It has been sung throughout the United States and Canada in
church, on the ranges, on radio, television, and 78 rpm records. It
is popular in two forms: one which is quite fluid and encompasses a
wide range of religious moods, depending on the stanzas used by a
particular singer; and the other a bona fide revivalist ballad where the
sequence of stanzas is stable, although there are variants within each
stanza sufficient to express feelings all the way from deism to fundamentalism. Its relationship to "Grand Roundup," No. 9 of this collection, is to be noted.

Here we present two integral texts to illustrate typical ways in
which this song is actually sung, and a composite text in which all
stanzas encountered, and significant variants, are given. (Text A: W.
S. James, *Cow-Boy Life in Texas,* Chicago: Donohue, Henneberry &
Co., 1893, pp. 212-213. Text B: Letter from Mrs. M. N. Perkins,
Perkinsville, Arizona, to J. Frank Dobie, May 21, 1930 [FAC II 125].
Melody: Library of Congress record 543B, sung by San Angelo Cow-
boy Quartet, Texas.)

Text A. *Last Round-Up*

When I think of the last great round-up
    On the eve of Eternity's dawn,
I think of the host of cow-boys
    Who have been with us here and have gone,

Roll On Dogies

Last night as I lay on the prai - rie ——

—— look - ing up at the stars in the sky, ——

—— I won - der if ev - er a cow-boy ——

—— would get to that sweet bye and bye. ——

Oh yes there will be a great round - up ——

—— where cow - boys like cat - tle will stand. ——

To be "cut" by the Rid - er of Judg - ment,

—— Who is post - ed and knows ev - ery brand. ——

—— Bring back, Bring back, Oh bring back my

cow - boy to me, to me. Bring back, bring

back, Oh bring back my cow - boy to me.

And I wonder if any will greet me
    On the sands of the evergreen shore;
With a hearty "God bless you, old fellow,"
    That I've met with so often before.

I think of the big-hearted fellows
    Who will divide with you blanket and bread,
With a piece of stray beef well roasted,
    And charge for it never a "red."
I often look upward and wonder,
    If the green fields will seem half so fair;
If any the wrong trail have taken
    And fail to "be in" over there.

For the trail that leads down to perdition
    Is paved all the way with good deeds;
But in the great round-up of ages,
    Dear boys, this won't answer your needs.
But the way to green pastures, though narrow,
    Leads straight to the home in the sky;
And Jesus will give you the passports
    To the land of the sweet by-and-by.

For the Savior has taken the contract
    To deliver all those who believe,
At the headquarters ranch of His Father,
    In the great range where none can deceive.
The Inspector will stand at the gate-way,
    And the herd, one and all must go by;
The round-up by the angels of judgment
    Must pass 'neath His all-searching eye.

No maverick or slick will be tallied
    In the great Book of Life in His home,
For He knows all the brands and the ear-marks
    That down through the ages have come.
But along with the strays and the sleepers
    The tailings must turn from the gate;
No road brand to gain them admission,
    But the awful sad cry "Too late!"

For the trail that leads down to perdition
    Is paved all the way with good deeds;

But in the great round-up of ages,
  Dear boys, this won't answer your needs.
But the way to green pastures, though narrow,
  Leads straight to the home in the sky;
And Jesus will give you the passports
  To the land of the sweet by-and-by.

Text B. *The Cowboy's Vision*

Last night as I lay on the prairie,
  Looking up to the stars in the sky,
I wonder if ever a cowboy
  Would get to that Sweet bye and bye.

Oh yes, there will be a great roundup
  Where cowboys like cattle will stand
To be "cut" by the Rider of Judgment,
  Who is posted and knows every brand.

        Bring back, bring back,
          Oh bring back my cowboy to me.
        Bring back, bring back,
          Oh bring back my cowboy to me.

The canyons and gorges are many
  And "dogies" go often astray
But the pale-horsed rider will gather
  Everyone to that great judgment day.

In that day of the great final judgment,
  When we all come around the white throne,
How happy will be every cowboy,
  To whom the Lord sayeth "Well done."

How sad, as we come to that roundup
  If our hearts do not have the right brand,
For no "maverick" or "stray" in the judgment
  Will ever be able to stand.

Then my brother, let's come to the branding,
  Our owner is calling today,
If he touches and blesses and owns you
  You'll be glad in that great judgment day.

Composite Text

Last night as I lay on the prairie
    And looked at the stars in the sky
I wondered if ever a cowboy
    Would drift to that sweet by and by.
             *

Tonight as I ride over the prairies
    And gaze at the great western sky
I wonder if ever a cowboy
    Will drift to the sweet by and by.
         *   *   *

They say there will be a great round-up
    And cowboys, like dogies, will stand
To be mavericked by the Riders of Judgment
    Who are posted and know every brand.
             *

I hear there's to be a grand round up
    Where cow-boys with others must stand
To be cut out by the riders of judgment
    Who are posted and know all the brands.
             *

When I think of the last great round-up
    On the eve of Eternity's dawn,
I think of the host of cow-boys
    Who have been with us here and have gone.
         *   *   *

The trail to that great mystic region
    Is narrow and dim so they say
While the one that leads down to perdition
    Is posted and blazed all the way.
             *

The canyons and gorges are many
    And "dogies" go often astray
But the pale-horsed rider will gather
    Everyone to that great judgment day.
             *

For the trail that leads down to perdition
    Is paved all the way with good deeds;
But in the great round-up of ages,
    Dear boys, this won't answer your needs.
             *

But the way to green pastures, though narrow,

Leads straight to the home in the sky;
And Jesus will give you the passports
   To the land of the sweet by-and-by.
* * *

I wonder if ever a cowboy
   Stood ready for that Judgment Day
And could say to the Boss of the Riders,
   "I'm ready, come drive me away."
*

In the day of the great final judgment
   When we all come around the white throne
How happy will be every cowboy
   To whom the Lord sayeth, "Well done."
*

On the final day of Judgment
   When the range boss cuts out the strays,
Will he leave any hard shooting gunmen
   To go to that straight narrow way?
*

I wonder if at the last day some cow-boy
   Un-branded and un-claimed should stand
Would he be mavericked by those riders of judgment
   Who are posted and know all the brands?
*

And I wonder if any will greet me
   On the sands of the evergreen shore;
With a hearty "God bless you, old fellow,"
   That I've met with so often before.
*

I think of the big-hearted fellows
   Who will divide with you blanket and bread,
With a piece of stray beef well roasted,
   And charge for it never a "red."
* * *

For they, like the cows that are locoed,
   Stampede at the sight of a hand,
Are dragged with a rope to the round-up
   Or get marked with some crooked man's brand.
*

For they're all like the cows from the "Jimpsons"
   That get scart at the sight of a hand
And have to be dragged to the round-up
   Or get put in some crooked man's brand.

— 72 —

I know there's many a stray cowboy
    Who'll be lost at the great final sale
When he might have gone in green pastures
    Had he known of the dim narrow trail.
        *

Whose fault is it then that so many
    Go astray on this wild range and fail
Who might have been rich and had plenty
    Had they known of the dim narrow trail.
        * * *

And I'm scared that I'll be a stray yearling—
    A maverick, unbranded on high—
And get cut in the bunch wtih the "rusties"
    When the Boss of the Riders goes by.
        *

Perhaps there will be a stray cowboy
    Unbranded by anyone nigh,
Who'll be cut by the riders of judgment
    And shipped to the sweet by and by.
        * * *

They tell of another big owner
    Who's ne'er overstocked, so they say
But who always makes room for the sinner
    Who drifts from the straight narrow way.
        * * *

They say he will never forget you
    That he knows every action and look
So for safety you'd better get branded
    Have your name in his big Tally Book.
        *

Oh, they say that the boss is a-coming
    To rope and to brand and earmark
And will take all the cuts back to Judgment
    To be registered in his great Tally Book.
        *

For the Savior has taken the contract
    To deliver all those who believe,
At the headquarters ranch of His Father,
    In the great range where none can deceive.
        *

No maverick or slick will be tallied
    In the great Book of Life in His home,

For He knows all the brands and the ear-marks
    That down through the ages have come.
             *

But along with the strays and the sleepers
    The tailings must turn from the gate;
No road brand to gain them admission,
    But the awful sad cry "Too late!"
          * * *

So 'haps there will be one stray cowboy
    Unspotted, unseen by an eye
That'll be roped by the riders of justice
    And shipped to the sweet by and by.
          * * *

I watched and I waited for Jesus
    But then for the light could I see
I wondered if Jesus, my redeemer
    Could save a poor sinner like me.
          * * *

Then my brother, let's come to the branding
    Our owner is calling today
If he touches and blesses and owns you
    You'll be glad in that great judgment day.
          * * *

Refrains:
    Roll on, roll on,
        Roll on, little dogies, roll on, roll on,
    Roll on, roll on,
        Roll on, little dogies, roll on.
          *

    Oh, bring back, bring back,
        Bring back my night horse to me
    Oh, bring back, bring back,
        Bring back my night horse to me.
          *

    Bring back, bring back,
        Oh bring back my cowboy to me.
    Bring back, bring back,
        Oh bring back my cowboy to me.
          *

    How sad as we come to that roundup
        If our hearts do not have the right brand
    For no "maverick" or "stray" in the judgment
        Will ever be able to stand.

> Will there be any cowboys in Heaven
> And bad broncs or steers we may ride?
> Will there be any campfires or cactus
> Over there on that great divide?

No. 30. *Home Corral*

This is a parody of "Grand Roundup," a meditation upon the comforts of life in the next world by a cowboy on night herd. (Hendren 46.)

> Sometimes when on night guard I'm riding
> And the stars are agleam in the sky
> Like millions of wee little candles
> That glimmer and sparkle on high
>
> I wonder if up there among them
> Are streets that are shining with gold,
> And if it's as pretty a country
> As all the Sky Pilot's have told.
>
> And sometimes I wonder and wonder
> If over that lone great divide
> I'll meet with my pals who have journeyed
> Across to that dim other side.
>
> If ever the great starry ranges
> Someday in the future I too
> Shall ride on a heavenly broncho
> When earth's final roundup is through.
>
> They tell us no storms nor blizzards
> Blow over that moon scattered range,
> That is always and always like summer,
> A land where there's never a change.
>
> At night when I lay in my blanket
> And the stars would cast over me a spell
> I seem to look on the glories
> That lie in that Great Home Corral.

No. 31. *Cowboy's Mother*

This is another parody to "Grand Roundup," the speculation of a cowboy who hankers to be reunited with his mother in the life beyond the grave. (Tex Fletcher, *"The Lonely Cowboy" Song Book,* New York, 1940, pp. 22-23.)

> Last night as I rode on the prairie,
>   Under the bright western sky
> I thought I heard mother a callin',
>   From the land of the sweet by and by,
> It wasn't the moon in the valley,
>   Making her shadow so clear
> Twas only the mind of a Cowboy
>   Thinking his mother was near.
>
> It sounded like I've heard her callin',
>   Like other times I have known
> Callin' as if she were guiding
>   My horse when I'm riding alone.
> I wonder if up there in Heaven,
>   She'll meet me when my life is o'er
> And lead to the ranch of the Father
>   Who lives on the bright golden shore.
>
> I know that Old Paint will be happy,
>   When our work on earth is done
> To ride on the trail up to Heaven,
>   At the set of the bright western sun.

No. 32. *The Last Ride*

This is a folksy homily in ballad form. A tenderfoot (pilgrim) is thrown and killed by a horse named "Old Nick." Others must be warned against a horse so mean. (Hendren 1252.)

> It was a tenderfoot, a youthful lad,
> Who came to the West the first chance he had,
> He was tired of knocking about in town,
> So he thought he'd go west and look around.
>
> He went to visit a ranch in the West,
> One of the roughest and toughest and best,
> The cowboys taught him how to rope and ride,
> Till the young tenderfoot was full of self pride.
>
> Now he said to himself one day,
> I'm sure I can ride the boss's bay;
> But that Old Bay was a wicked one,
> Full of onery tricks and all sorts of fun.

The pilgrim roped and caught the bay,
Saddled it up, then rode away;
And the bay he knew that his load was strange,
It was never so light on his home range.

The bronco's name, it was Old Nick,
And suddenly it began to buck and kick;
The pilgrim held on with all his might,
He never did think that Bay would fight.

The Bay, he comes to a rugged spot,
Into the air the tenderfoot shot;
Now that the bay was rid of its load,
It went snorting back on the homeward road.

The tenderfoot fell on a jagged rock,
Lay there limp from the terrible shock;
His neck was broken, no more he said,
His life was gone, he lay there dead.

The boss came in from his work that day,
He looked around and saw his bay;
Standing by the corral with his saddle on,
He looked for the pilgrim but he was gone.

An idea flashed thru the boss's head,
Could it be possible the pilgrim was dead?
Would he ride Old Nick on the lonesome range,
Here was something mysterious and strange.

He told his cowboys to comb the range around,
And not come back till the tenderfoot was found,
But they saw him lying all limp and still,
And knew that he'd gone over the hill.

They saw the prints of the boss's Old Nick,
And they knew that he had done his trick;
"That was his last ride," sadly said the boss,
"I wish I had a-warned him about that hoss."

The tenderfoot was laid away to rest,
His life was gone but his soul was blessed.
The cowboys will remember that pilgrim's sad fate,
And warn all others before it's too late.

Part VI

Prayers and Homiletic Songs and Verse

Several types of lyrical expression are used by revivalist sects: ballads, songs, poems, hymns, prayers, sermons. However, as is illustrated by the texts of this study, the distinctions between them are not always clearly drawn, except when they are actually being used in the cult.

Although all of the texts cited in this study come to us fom print, from manuscripts, or from oral sources outside the cult, any one of them could well have found a place in the cult sometime, somewhere. However, their real vitality as specimens of folk expression is seen typically in less formal, personalized renditions. Some are prayers largely because they are called prayers, or because they address God directly. Others are simply homiletic pieces which defend traditional Christian values in the Western idiom.

No. 33. *A Range Rider's Appeal (The Cowboy's Prayer)*

This is a cowman's prayer. He asks for the things we all ask for, but in the idiom of the range: protection from dangers of life on earth, from blasphemous speech, from sinful behavior; for God's presence in adversity, beautiful surroundings, adherence to the Golden Rule, to shun the curse of Cain, safe conduct to heaven. This seems to be a parody of the hymn "Guide Me O, Thou Great Jehovah," melody of which we give. (Text A: Hendren 324. Text B: PNFQ 86. Melody: *The Broadman Hymnal,* B. B. McKinney, ed., Nashville, Tennessee: Broadman Press, 1940, p. 181.)

Text A. *A Range Rider's Appeal*

Guide me, Lord, when I am riding
    Crost the dusty range out there,
From the dangers that are hiding
    On the trails so bleak and bare.
Keep my stumblin' feet from walkin'
    In the quicksands of distress,
And my outlawed tongue from talkin'
    Locoed words of foolishness.

Guide Me, O Thou Great Jehovah

Guard me, Lord when I'm a - rid - in' 'Crost the dust - y trail out there, From the dan - gers that are hid - in' on the trail so bleak and bare.

When around the herd I'm moggin'
    In the darkness of the night,
Or acrost lone mesa joggin'
    With no one but you in sight,
Won't you ride, dear Lord, beside me,
    When I see the danger sign,
And thru storm and stampede guide me
    With your hand a-hold of mine.

May the rope o' sin ne'er trip me
    When for fun to town I go,
Let the devil's herders skip me
    In their round up there below.
May my trails be decked with beauty,
    With the blossoms of your love,
May I see and do my duty
    Ere I ride the range above.

Let me treat my foes with kindness,
    May my hands from blood be free.

May I never thru sheer blindness
    Never get the brand o' Cain on me.
On the range of Glory feed me,
    Guide me o'er draw and swell,
And at last to heaven lead me
    Up in the Home Corral.

Text B.   *The Cowboy's Prayer*

Guard me, Lord, when I'm a-ridin',
    'Crost the dusty trail out there,
From the dangers that are hidin'
    On the trail so bleak and bare.

Keep my stumblin' feet from walkin'
    In the quicksands of distrust,
And my outlaw tongue from talkin'
    Locoed words of foolishness.

When around the herd I'm moggin'
    On a dark and stormy night,
Or acrost the mesa joggin'
    With no one but you in sight,

Won't you ride, dear Lord, beside me
    When I see the danger sign?
An' through storm an' stampede guide me
    With your hand a-holdin' mine.

May the ropes of sin ne'er trip me
    When to town for fun I go;
May the devil's herders skip me
    In their roundup here below.

May the trail be decked in beauty
    With blossoms of your love,
May I see an' do my duty
    Ere I ride the range above.

Let me treat my foes with kindness,
    May my hands from blood be free;
Let me never through sheer blindness
    Get the brand of Cain on me.

On the range of Glory feed me,
An' at last to heaven lead me,
Up into the home corral.

No. 34.   *A Cowboy's Prayer*

This is one of the greatest lyrical expressions in the cowboy mode. The range setting, cowboy values and commitments, are seen as the highest reality achievable by man. It was written by Charles Badger Clark when he was working on a ranch near Tombstone, Arizona, and first published in *The Pacific Monthly* for December, 1906. We quote it from his volume of verse, *Sun and Saddle Leather,* Boston: Richard G. Badger, 1922, pp. 50-51. (Melody: *Marc Williams Collection of Favorite Songs,* New York: Bob Miller, Inc., 1937, pp. 4-5.)

Oh Lord, I've never lived where churches grow.
   I love creation better as it stood
That day You finished it so long ago
   And looked upon Your work and called it good.
I know that others find You in the light
   That's sifted down through tinted window panes,
And yet I seem to feel You near tonight
   In this dim, quiet starlight on the plains.

I thank You, Lord, that I am placed so well,
   That You have made my freedom so complete;
That I'm no slave of whistle, clock or bell,
   Nor weak-eyed prisoner of wall and street.
Just let me live my life as I've begun
   And give me work that's open to the sky;
Make me a pardner of the wind and sun,
   And I won't ask a life that's soft or high.

Let me be easy on the man that's down;
   Let me be square and generous with all.
I'm careless sometimes, Lord, when I'm in town,
   But never let 'em say I'm mean or small!
Make me as big and open as the plains,
   As honest as the hawse between my knees,
Clean as the wind that blows behind the rains,
   Free as the hawk that circles down the breeze!

A Cowboy's Prayer

Lord, I've nev-er lived where church-es grow. I love Cre-a-tion bet-ter as it stood, That day you fin-ished it so long a-go, And looked up-on your work and called it good. I know that oth-ers find you in the light That's sift-ed down through tint-ed win-dow panes, And yet I seem to feel you near to-night In this dim, qui-et star-light on the plain.

Forgive me, Lord, if sometimes I forget.
  You know about the reasons that are hid.
You understand the things that gall and fret;
  You know me better than my mother did.
Just keep an eye on all that's done and said
  And right me, sometimes, when I turn aside,
And guide me on the long, dim trail ahead
  That stretches upward toward the Great Divide.

No. 35. *The Cowman's Prayer*

This cowman's request forms a sharp contrast with the preceding item. Here the petition is openly materialistic: verdant forage, water for the cattle, safety from scourge and storm, good prices for beef. But the request of the last stanza for twin births in lieu of the single birth typical for cattle has an ironic twist which suggests that the whole petition is made with tongue in cheek. (Text: *Socorro* [New Mexico] *Bullion*, October 30, 1886, as quoted by Clifford Westermeier, *Trailing the Cowboy*, Caldwell, Idaho: Caxton Printers, 1955, pp. 265-266. Melody: Victor 21402, Carl T. Sprague.)

Now, O Lord, please lend Thine ear,
The prayer of the cattle man to hear;
No doubt many prayers to Thee seem strange
But won't you bless our cattle range?

Bless the round-up, year by year,
And don't forget the growing steer;
Water the land with brooks and rills,
For my cattle that roam on a thousand hills.

Now, O Lord, won't you be good,
And give our stock plenty of food;
And to avert a winter's woe,
Give Italian skies and little snow.

Prairie fires won't you please stop?
Let thunder roll and water drop;
It frightens me to see the smoke—
Unless it's stopped I'll go dead broke.

As you, O Lord, my herds behold—
Which represents a sack of gold—

I think at least five cents per pound
Should be the price of beef the year 'round.

One thing more and then I'm through—
Instead of one calf, give my cows two,
I may pray different than other men,
Still I've had my say, and now Amen!

The Cowman's Prayer

Now, O Lord, please lend Thine ear, The
prayer of the cat - tle man to hear; No
doubt man - y prayers to Thee seem strange But
won't you bless our cat - tle range?

No. 36.   *The Cowboy's Heaven*

This plodding and clumsy poem equates the cowboy's life with life eternal on a point by point basis. It is one of several cowboy parodies of Whittier's "Backward, Turn Backward." As other pieces in this collection testify, the cowboys are not apt to be happy at the prospect of a heaven as sterile as it was typically portrayed. (Jules Verne Allen, *Cowboy Lore,* San Antonio: Naylor Company, 1933, pp. 14-15.)

Onward, flow onward, time never will cease,
While earth and its beauties will gradually decrease;
When all is ended and life is no more,
O where will the spirit of the cowboy go?

His human ambitions in struggles and strife,
Strengthens his soul for the spiritual life;
For right against evil he has always stood,
Rejecting temptation for the true and the good.

With a humble confession to Christ he yields all,
Preparing his soul for Eternity's call;
His spirit will mount high in the celestial day,
While the body will return to mineral and clay.

The weak human mind cannot understand,
The change from earth to the Heavenly Land;
The broad open prairies that before him rolled,
Are replaced in heaven by streets of pure gold.

The old cow horse that he rode alone,
Will be given up for a seat on the Throne;
The Angels' songs of beautiful words,
Will take the place of the lowing herds.

The old *sombrero* will not be known,
For a crown in heaven by the redeemed is worn;
No longer he will drink from the rocks and sod,
As his thirst will be quenched from the throne of God.

The old cloth tent will not be there,
As the skies of heaven are always fair;
The power of God will guide all his works,
And take the place of lariats and quirts.

The useful raincoat when not worn on the back,
Was tied behind the saddle with all kinds of pack,
But this dear old relic is nothing to compare,
With the spotless white robes the cowboys will wear.

His slumbers are deep and never disturbed,
By the lowing and running of a stampeded herd;
No early call at rise of sun,
To begin hard work with a long day's run.

The bacon that sizzled in the old black pan,
And the coffee that boiled in the little tin can,

— 85 —

Will be of no value on which to feed,
For the tree of life will supply every need.

The pleasures of earth cannot compare,
With the ease and comfort and spiritual care,
Filled with the beauty of heavenly glare,
Awaiting the cowboy when he gets there.

The saved cowboy will not be alone,
True comrades will met him around the Throne,
Then after all for what is life given,
Nothing more than to prepare for heaven.

No. 37.   *A Cowboy at Church*

A cowboy in town, by sheer chance on a Sunday, responds to the
church bell's call and enters, where a snobbish throng makes him feel
unwanted. Yet salvation is for the genuinely good and there may be
some surprises when the brands are finally read! (Text: JL 179.
Melody: Bluebird B6258B, Carl T. Sprague.)

Some time ago, two weeks or more, if I remember well
I found myself in town and thought I'd knock around a spell
When all at once I heard the bell and didn't know it was Sunday,
For on the plains we scarcely know Sunday from Monday.

A-calling all the people from the highways and the hedges,
And all the reckless throng that tread ruin's ragged edges,
To come and hear the pastor tell salvation's touching story
And how the new road misses hell and leads you straight to glory.

I started by the chapel door, but something urged me in
And told me not to spend God's day in revelry and sin.
I don't go much on sentiment, but tears came to my eyes,
It seemed just like my mother's voice was speaking from the skies.

I thought how often she had gone with little Sis and me
When I was but a lad way back in Tennessee.
It never once occurred to me, although not being dressed
In Sunday rig, but carelessly I went in with the rest.

You should have seen the smiles and shrugs as I went walking in
As though they thought my leggings worse than moral guilt and sin.

A Cowboy at Church

Some time a - go, two weeks or more, if I re - mem - ber well I found my self in town and thought I'd knock a - round a spell When all at once I heard the bell and did - n't know it was Sun - day, For on the plains we scarce - ly know a Sun - day from a Mon - day.

Although the honest parson in his vestry garb arrayed
Was dressed the same as I was—in the trappings of his trade.

The good man prayed for all the world and all it motley crew,
For pagan, Hindu, sinners, Turk, and unbelieving Jew.
Though the congregation doubtless thought that the cowboys as a race
Were kind of moral centaurs with no valid claim to grace.

Is it very strange that cowboys are a rough and reckless crew
When their garb forbids their doing right as Christian people do?
That they frequent scenes of revelry where death is bought and sold
Where at least they get a welcome, though it is prompted by their gold?

Stranger, did it never strike you when the winter days are gone
And the mortal grass is springing up to meet the judgment sun
And we tend mighty round-ups, when according to the word
The angel cowboy of the Lord will cut the human herd?

That a heap of stock that's lowly now around the Master's pen
And feeding at his fodder stack will have the brand picked then
And brands that while the hair was long looked like the letter G
Will prove to be the devil and the brand was letter D.

While many a longhorn coaster, I mean just so to speak,
That hasn't had the adventure of the range in Gospel Creek
Will get to crop the herbage in the pasture of the Lord
If the letter G showed up beneath the devil's checker board.

No. 38.   *Rattlin' Joe's Prayer*

A proper burial, on the open ranges, was of great concern to the cowboys, and many of their songs treat this crisis. Monte Bill was luckier than most, Rattlin' Joe being present and able to give him a proper send-off with a deck of playing cards serving as text. Edward L. Saslow, of the University of California at Berkeley, informs us that a progenitor of "The Prayer Book in Cards," or "Rattlin' Joe's Prayer," appears in the diary of the Rev. John Tomlinson, entry for April 8, 1717, in *Six North Country Diaries,* Publs. of the Surtees Soc., CXVIII (1910), p. 65. (Text: JL 326.)

> Just pile on some more o' them pine knots
> > And squat yourself down on this skin,
> And Shorty, let up on your growlin',
> > The boys are all tired of your chin.
> Alleghany, just pass round the bottle,
> > And give the lads all a square drink,
> And soon as you're saddled I'll tell you
> > A yarn that'll please yuh, I think.
>
> 'Twas in the year of eighteen hundred and eighty,
> > A day in the bright month of June,
> When the Angel of Death from the round-up,
> > Snatched Monte Bill, known as McCune,
> Wild Bill whar a favorite among us
> > In spite of the trade which he had,

Which whar gamblin'; but don't you forget it,
 He often made weary hearts glad.

And, pards, while he lay in that coffin,
 Which we hewed from the trunk o' a tree,
His face whar as calm as an angel's
 And white as an angel's could be.
And there's where the trouble started, pards,
 For there whar no gospel sharps in the camp,
And Joe says, "We can't drop him this way,
 Without no directions or stamps."

Then up spoke old Sandy McGregor,
 "Looky yar, mates, I'm regular dead stuck,
I can hold no hand at religion,
 And I'm feared Bill's run in out o' luck.
If I knowed a darn thing about praying,
 I'd chip in and say him a mass,
But I ain't got no show in the layout;
 I can't beat the game so I pass."

Rattlin' Joe whar the next o' the speakers,
 And he were a friend o' the dead,
The salt water stood in his peepers,
 And these were the words that he said:
"Boys, you know I ain't any Christian,
 And I'll gamble the good Lord don't know
There ever lived such a rooster as I am,
 But once there whar a time long ago,

"When I whar a kid I remember
 My old mother sent me to school,
To the little brown church every Sunday
 Whar they said I was dumb as a mule.
And I reckon I've nearly forgotten
 About all that I ever knew,
But still if you'll drop to my racket,
 I'll show you just what I can do.

"Just hand me them cards off the bar,
 And I'll show you my Bible," said Joseph.
"I'll convince yuh it is a Bible,"
 And he went to work shufflin' the pack.

— 89 —

He spread out the cards on the table
    And began kinder pious-like: "Pards,
If you'll just choose your racket and listen,
    I'll show you the prayer book in cards.

"The ace that reminds us of one God,
    The deuce of Father and Son,
The trey of Father, Son, Holy Ghost,
    For you see all them three are but one.
The four spot is Matthew, Mark, Luke, and John;
    The five spot, the five virgins who trimmed
Their lamps while it was yet day,
    And the five foolish virgins who sinned.

"The six spot, in six days the Lord made the world,
    The sea, and the stars in heaven,
He saw it whar good what he'd made, so He said,
    'I'll just go rest on the seven.'
The eight spot is Noah, his wife, and three sons,
    And Noah's three sons had their wives.
God loved the whole mob, so He bid 'em embark;
    In a freshet He saved all their lives.

"The nine were the lepers of Biblical fame,
    A repulsive and hideous squad,
The ten are the Holy Commandments which came
    To us perishin' creatures from God.
The queen war of Sheba in old Bible times,
    The king represents old King Sol.
She brought in a hundred young folks, boys and girls,
    To the king in his government hall.

"They was all dressed alike, and she asked the old boy,
    (She'd put up his wisdom as bosh),
Which were boys and which was girls. Old Sol said,
    "How dirty their hands! Make 'em wash."
And then he showed Sheba the boys only washed
    Their hands and part of their wrists
While the girls just went up to their elbows in suds.
    Sheba weakened and shook the King's fists.

"Now the knave, that's the Devil, and God if you please,
    Just keep his hands off'un poor Bill,

And now lads, just drop on your knees for a while
    Till I draw and perhaps I can fill
And having no Bible, I'll pray on the cards,
    For I've showed yuh they're all on the square,
And I think God'll cotton to all that I say
    If I'm only sincere in the prayer.

"Just give him a corner, good Lord, not on stocks
    Fur I ain't such a darned fool as that
To ask you for anything worldly fur Bill
    'Cause you know me down there fur a flat.
I'm lost on the rules of your game, but I'll ask
    Fur a seat fur him back o' the throne
And I'll bet my whole stack, the boy'll behave
    If your angels just let him alone.

"There's nothing bad about him unless he gets riled;
    The boys'll all back me in that,
But if anyone treads on his corns, then you bet
    He'll fight at the drop o' a hat.
Just don't let your angels run over him, Lord,
    Nor shut off all at once on his drink,
Break him in kinda gentle and mild at the start,
    And he'll give you no trouble, I think.

"And couldn't you give him a pack of old cards
    To amuse himself once in a while,
But I warn you right here not to bet on his game,
    Or he'll get right away with your pile.
And now, Lord, I hope you've took it all in
    And listened to all that I've said.
I know that my prayin' is jest a bit thin,
    But I've done all I kin fur the dead.

"And I hope I ain't troubled your Lordship too much,
    So I'll cheese it in asking again
That you don't let the 'Knave' get his hands on poor Bill.
    That's all, Lord, yours truly, amen."

No. 39. *The Hell-Bound Train*

This song, a favorite among range folk, is a kind of Western American dance of death, not unlike the ones carved above the portals of

Romanesque cathedrals. The drunken cowboy's imagination takes him on a razzle-dazzle train ride to the very portals of hell. He awakens in full awareness of his miscreant life and resolves to mend it.

Parodies of this song were sung by airmen in World War II (William Wallrich, *Air Force Airs,* New York: Duell, Sloan and Pearce, 1957, pp. 155-157.) It was a favorite, too, among temperance songs, having its analogue in "The Drunkard's Hell." (Text: PC-F 81, unidentified newspaper clipping. Melody: FMC I 974, sung by Phyllis Stocks and Evelyn Ward, Moab, Utah.)

The Hell-Bound Train

A Tex - as cow - boy lay down on a bar - room floor Hav - ing drunk — so much he could drink no more, So he fell a - sleep with a troub - led brain To dream that he rode on a hell - bound train.

Tom Gay lay down on the barroom floor,
Having drank so much he could drink no more.
So he fell asleep with a troubled brain
To dream that he rode on the hell-bound train.

The engine with blood was red and damp,
And brilliantly lit with a brimstone lamp;
An Imp, for fuel, was shoveling bones,
While the furnace rang with endless groans;

The boiler was filled with lager beer,
And the devil himself was the engineer.

The passengers made a motley crew—
Church member, atheist, Gentile, Jew;
Rich men in broadcloth, beggars in rags,
Handsome young ladies and withered old hags.
Yellow men, black men, red, brown and white—
And chained together—a horrible sight!
While the train dashed on at an awful pace,
And a hot wind scorched their hands and face.

Wilder and wilder the country grew,
As faster and faster the engine flew.
Louder and louder the thunder crashed,
Brighter and brighter the lightning flashed.
Hotter and hotter the air became,
Till the clothes were burnt from each quivering frame.
And in the distance there rose a yell—
"Ha ha!" croaked the devil, "we're nearing hell."

Then, Oh! how the passengers shrieked with pain,
And begged the devil to stop the train:
But he capered about and sang with glee,
And laughed and joked at their agony.
"My faithful friends, you have done my work
And the devil can never a pay day shirk;
You have bullied the weak, you have robbed the poor,
And the starving brother turned from the door.

"You have laid up gold where the canker rusts,
You gave free vent to your fleshly lusts;
You have justice scorned and corruption sown
So the devil himself must claim his own.
You have drunk and rioted, murdered and lied,
And mocked at God in your hell-born pride;
You have paid full fare so I will carry you through,
For it is only right that you get your due.

"The laborer always expects his hire,
So I'll land you safe in my lake of fire,
Where your flesh shall roast in the flames that roar,
And my imps torment you forever more."

When Tom awoke with an awful cry,
His clothes were soaked and his hair on high;
He prayed as he never prayed till that hour,
To be saved from drink and the devil's power,
And his vows and prayers were not made in vain
For he disembarked from that hell-bound train.

No. 40.　*A Cowboy's Prayer*

The following cowboy's prayer from a manuscript of J. Frank Dobie expresses the tempo, the mood, and the images which served range men best in their hours of confrontation with the hereafter. (FAC II 124.)

Oh Lord, round us up in one great round up
And rope us with the cords of love—
Brand us with the iron of truth
And mark us with the cross of Calvary—
So when we start on the last great drive
Grant that there shall not be any cut-backs
As we appear before the Head Boss
In the green Pastures of Eternal Reward.
Amen.

Part VII

Decline of the Genre

In song the cowboy metaphor endured for three or four decades after the fencing of the ranges and the motorization of the cowboys. The era of 78 rpm phonograph records and of radio broadcasts saw created a few of the best of the cowboy songs, and several of the worst: witness those that follow. Pseudo-cowboy songs infused with Christian moralization of the 1920's and '30's are legion. For the most part they evoke the open ranges and ranch routine in the vaguest possible way. Shall we conclude by saying simply that old cowboy songs never die, they just go away to Hollywood?

No. 41. *Stick Close to Your Bedding Ground*

This song evokes the two-legged critters in a revivalist's tent a bit more than it does real range cattle and the moments that precede a stampede. Still it gets down to the fundamental issues of life, retaining the essential cowboy images, though ranch folks would have wept indeed to hear an "ole mammy cow" told to "quit your moanin' round." (Text: Hendren 370. Melody: *World's Original Radio Jamboree Famous Songs,* Chicago: M. M. Cole Publishing Co., 1942, pp. 33-34.)

When the night is black and the storm clouds crack
　　Driving cattle wild with fear,
There's a lightning flash and a thunder crash
　　Then a mad stampede is near.
It's a cowboy's job to hold the mob
　　When the herd starts millin' round,
Then in voices strong you will hear this song
　　As the herd is bedded down.

　　　　Now hush your bawling, little dogies,
　　　　　　Be quiet now and settle down,
　　　　And you foolish old steers, ain't no sense to your fears,
　　　　　　Stick close to your bedding ground.
　　　　The flashin' lightning is the lantern
　　　　　　Of the big boss in the sky,
　　　　And the thunder is the noise of the boss and his boys
　　　　　　Ridin' herd at the ranch on High.

Stick Close to Your Bedding Ground

When the night is black and the storm clouds crack, Driving cat - tle wild with fear, There's a light - ing flash and thun - der crash, Then a mad stampede is near. It's a cow - boy's job to hold the mob When the herd starts mill - in' 'round. Then in voices strong you will hear this song As the herd is bed - ded down. Now hush your howl - in' lit - tle dog - gie, Be qui - et now and set - tle down, And you fool - ish old steers, Ain't no sense to your fears, Stick close to your bed - ding ground. The flash - in' lightin' is the

So wait for the sun, little dogie,
    For the sun and a bright new day,
Wait for the sun, little dogie,
    To chase the storm away.
Now hush your bawling, little dogie,
    Be quiet now and settle down
    [This line has an alternate reading:
    Ol' mammy cow quit your moanin' 'round,]
And you foolish old steers, ain't no sense to your fears,
    Stick close to your bedding ground.

Now a cowboy ain't a plaster saint
   With a golden harp and wings,
While angel songs and opera songs
   Ain't the kind the cowboy sings.
Yet his cheerful words will quiet herds
   And calm and safety bring,
Will meet the need when the herds stampede,
   So listen while he sings:

Refrain.

No. 42. *He's Gone Up the Trail*

Range folk never looked upon Buffalo Bill as anything but a showman. This fact alone marks this song as a synthetic product of ranges close to "Hollywood and Vine." (Text: PNFQ 187. Melody: *Sons of the Pioneers Original Songs of the Prairie,* Folio No. 3, Hollywood: American Music Co., c. 1937, pp. 46-47.)

There's gloom around the bunkhouse tonight,
   There's gloom 'round the old corral,
I said goodbye to a cowboy tonight,
   I said goodbye to my pal.

He's gone, he's gone up the trail,
   His old guitar is still.
He's gone to join the heavenly band
   That's led by Buffalo Bill.

Old Pinto's head is hanging low,
   He's missing the cowboy's song;
The moon is pale, it seems to know
   Tonight there's something wrong.

I'll lay my fiddle away to rest,
   To rest with his old guitar,
To never play until the day
   When I cross over the bar.

He's Gone, He's Gone Up the Trail

There's gloom a - round the ranch - house to night, There's gloom in the old cor - ral, —— My heart is blue and so lone - some too, I said, "Good - bye," to my pal. He's gone, he's gone up the trail, —— His old gui - tar is still, —— He's gone to join a Heav - en - ly band, That's led by Buf - fa - lo Bill. ——

No. 43. *Once I Lived a Happy Life*

This is a fairyland cowboy song which achieves its transcendental allusions from a fusion of the cowboy mode and Stephen Foster: Powder River Jack Lee and his wife Kitty, to whom we owe the song, rode the ranges during the '20's and '30's as minstrels and not as genuine cattle folk. The inept and exaggerated evocation of cow country life is as phony as a three-dollar bill. (Text: Hendren 1232. Melody: *Powder River Jack and Kitty Lee's Cowboy Song Book,* Butte, Montana: McKee Printing Co., 1938, pp. 62-63.)

> Once I lived a happy life, 'way out on the plain,
> Far from all the city strife with its grief and pain.

Once I Led a Happy Life

Once I led a hap-py life way out on the
plains, far a - way from cit - y strife, with its grief and
pain, with my bron - co for a friend, I was wild and free,
and I'm go - in' back a - gain, where I long to be.
Go - in' home, go-in' home where the coy-otes howl and the
cat - tle roam, go - in' home, go - in' home I'm
go - in' home to stay, where the skies are al - ways blue,
and where friends are ev - er true, ne - ver more,
will I roam, I'm go - in' go - in' home.

With my bronco for my friend I was wild and free,
And I'm going back again where I long to be.

Goin' home, goin' home,
Where coyotes howl and cattle roam.
Goin' home, goin' home, goin' home to stay,
Where the skies are always blue,
Where the friends are always true,
Never more will I roam, goin', goin' home.

Many hours I'd ride the range, happy all the while,
Never mind the weather change, take it with a smile.
With my good old forty-four hangin' by my side,
I'd go ridin' down the trail where the redskins hide.

Then at night I'd make my bed, blanket on the ground,
With my saddle for my head I would lay me down,
Listenin' to the sound of night, cattle grazin' near,
With the stars' protectin' light nothin' would I fear.

With the light of early dawn flamin' in the skies,
I would roll my blanket up, rub my sleepy eyes.
Boil my coffee in a can, make it good and strong,
Start another happy day with a cowboy song.

When the last great roundup comes on that judgment day,
And I'm headin' for the range where I'll never stray,
When they lay me down to rest on the lone prairie,
I will hear the angels sing soft and tenderly.

No. 44. *Drift Along Lonely Cowboy*

In this late-blooming cowboy song there's little left of the range and range cattle: just a rider and his horse and the Great Range beyond death. Its composition is attributed to Curley Fletcher, author of the famous "Strawberry Roan." (Text: Hendren 79. Melody: *Tex Ritter Mountain Ballads and Cowboy Songs*, Chicago: M. M. Cole Publishing Co., p. 22.)

In the far away heavens in distant blue skies,
High above in the bright gleaming sun,
Is a heaven of rest for the Great Master's guest
When the roundup on earth is all done.

Drift Along Lonely Cowboy

Thru ever green meadows the rider will stray
    In the flush of an eternal dawn
With the Boss by your side thru the heavens you'll ride
    Drift along, lonely cowboy, drift on.

Drift along, lonely cowboy, drift on to your new range,
    There's a chuckwagon camped there on high.

Old time friends you will find who once left you behind,
    And we'll all meet you there by and by.

The Boss of the roundup will lend you a hand,
    He'll be waiting for you in the dawn,
In the campfire's glow are old faces you'll know,
    Drift along, lonely cowboy, drift on.

No. 45.   *Do You Think There's a Prairie in Heaven?*

To perceive the evolution of the cowboy genre from its authentic range sources to the pseudo-cowboy of the mass media, one has but to compare this song with "The Cowboy's Soliloquy," No. 2 of this collection. The sharp configurations of the range and confrontation with authentic range life are dimmed in a hazy suggestion of the out-of-doors and salvation in the open air. Moreover, no genuine puncher would be caught dead talking to his horse, save in four-letter words. (Hendren 732.)

It was night on the lone western prairie,
    The western stars shone so bright,
A lonesome cowboy sat by the campfire
    Wondering that very night
Old Paint seemed to understand,
    He whispered, "Old Pal, I wonder
What it's like in the Promised Land.

"Do you think there is a prairie in heaven?
    Where we can roam by and by,
We'd never be happy in heaven
    Without this western sky.
They say it's a land of great promise
    And no other place can compare,
But if there's no prairie in heaven
    We'd never be happy up there.

"Do you think there is a prairie in heaven
    Where the coyotes howl and play?
Can we make our beds 'neath the starlight
    And sleep till the break of day?
They say in the great promised kingdom
    One never has worries or care,
But if there's no prairie in heaven
    We'd never be happy up there."

No. 46. *Cowboy's Prayer at Twilight*

The mood and sentiment of western evangelism are present here, but the cowboy images are dimmed by the light of "that big Texas moon," now diffused by the aroma of oil. (Text and melody: *Stuart Hamblen and His Lucky Stars,* Chicago: M. M. Cole Publishing Co., 1942, pp. 38-39.)

Cowboy's Prayer at Twilight

flow - ers that bloom on the sand, For the warm des - ert sun and the

cool moun - tain stream for all these my thanks for your

bless - ings so grand, God, please don't ev - er change the

prai - rie, Leave it just as it is to - day. For the

light of this big Tex - as moon, out shines stars from the Great White

Way. Please Lord, grant me now just this one small re - quest. Watch

o - ver my do - gies to - night, Let the camp - fire burn low as the

shad - ows grow dim and please ans - wer a cow - boy's pray'r at twi - light.

When a cowboy's day is over and the sun sinks in the West,
When the dogies all are tended then a cowboy goes to rest,
He beds down beside the campfire 'neath a western Texas sky,
And this pray'r you'll hear him whisper to the breezes lullaby.

> Dear Lord, I ain't much on them big fancy words
> And I don't much know how to pray;
> But my heart is so filled with contentment and peace
> I reckon you know what I'm tryin' to say.
> I'm thankful to you for the prairies so fair,
> And flowers that bloom on the sand,

For the warm desert sun and the cool mountain stream
 For all these my thanks for your blessings so grand.
God, please don't ever change the prairie,
 Leave it just as it is today,
For the light of this big Texas moon,
 Outshines stars from "The Great White Way."
Please Lord, grant me now just this one small request
 "Watch over my dogies tonight"
Let the campfire burn low as the shadows grow dim
 And please answer a cowboy's pray'r at twilight.

No. 47. *A Cowboy's Prayer*

  In this, and many pseudo-cowboy songs of the early '30's, the range and real cowpunching are about gone, leaving little but nostalgia and a plea for salvation on the one hand, and dreams of "the gal I love" on the other, with the scale slightly tipped toward the latter. The horse, the dogies, and the prairie are but fossil images of a previous era. (Hendren 1024.)

The cattle's bedded down on the prairie
 The sun is hangin' low in the west
Ol' Pinto is tired and weary
 And he's needin' his rest.
We've been on the range all day,
 So tonight, O Lord, I pray:

  Let me lay and rest under western skies,
   Protect me from all harm,
  Keep your guiding light on me tonight
   Lord, that's just a Cowboy's prayer.
  Let the dogies dream of a pasture green,
   Where they don't burn hide or hair,
  Watch o'er every stray till the break of day,
   Lord, that's just a cowboy's prayer.
  You can use my saddle and my lariat
   To round up the cattle that stray,
  You could use old Pinto, but he's tired and sore,
   We've been ridin' hard all day.
  Blanket me with stars and the moon above,
   Keep your watch from away up there,
  Let me dream tonight of the gal I love,
   Lord, that's just a cowboy's prayer.

No. 48. *Cowboy's Heaven*

The image of a departed cowboy whistling up his pony from a cloud pasture in heaven, reporting to the Range Boss for duty, riding circle on the stars and wrangling the critters of the Milky Way, seems a bit over-drawn. But must we deny simple folk their excursions amidst the cosmic just because their metaphors are fenced in? (Text and melody: Gramaphone Ltd., Sydney [Australia] N.S.W., March 1933: Gene Autry and Jimmy Long.)

Cowboy's Heaven

Tonight I'm a tired weary cowboy,
    I've been in the saddle all day
Searching the hills and the valleys
    For the cattle that strayed away.
Old Paint is tired and leg-weary,
    His feet are broken and sore.
But some day our work will be over
    And we'll ride on that other shore.

Lying wrapped up in my blankets,
    Looking straight up at the sky,
Watching the bright stars a twinkling
    Away up there on high,
Seems sometimes maybe they see me
    And maybe they'll understand,
For they may be the drove of cowpunchers
    Gone to that Promised Land.

When I get 'way up there yonder
    I'll whistle softly and low,
And my Old Paint horse will come running
    From a passing cloud pasture, I know.
I'll give him a handful of sugar
    And watch him say thanks with his eye,
I'll mount and then we'll be ready
    To report to the Range Boss on high.

They'll be work up there a plenty
    For a good old cowpuncher some day,
Keeping straight shooting stars in the pastures,
    Riding herd on the Milky Way.
The comets they all must be mavericked
    That'll have to be marked with His brand,
You bet me and Old Paint will be happy
    On the range in the Promised Land.

No. 49. *The Big Ranch Boss*

A lesson of preparedness to meet God and the Day of Judgment is given, using those tags of the cowboy mode which are accessible alike to "billies" of country and city. (Hendren 934.)

    When the big ranch Boss comes riding by
    In splender rare in the sky,

When the big ranch Boss comes riding by
Will you be there on high?

There he'll judge every brand
From each section of the land
In that big round up
That last big roundup.

Where he'll pick the best
That can stand the test
In the big roundup, up there
When the big ranch Boss comes riding by
Will you be there?

When the big ranch Boss comes riding by
On the last trail in the sky
When the big ranch Boss comes riding by
Oh will you fail on high?

Where His pastures are green
Everything is serene
In heaven's westland
Will you wear his brand?

Will you share blessings rare
Share those blessings there
In the big round up, up there
When the big ranch Boss comes riding by
Will you be there?

Index of Titles and First Lines

Index (*Continued*)

Index (Continued)

Index (Continued)